LIVES&
LEGACIES

Frantz Fanon

SERIES EDITOR: BARBARA LEAH ELLIS

PATRICK EHLEN

Frantz Fanon

A Spiritual Biography

A Crossroad 8th Avenue Book
The Crossroad Publishing Company
New York

The Crossroad Publishing Company
481 Eighth Avenue, Suite 1550
New York, NY 10001

First published in 2000 by The Crossroad Publishing Company

LIBRARY OF CONGRESS CATALOGING-IN-PUBLICATION DATA
Ehlen, Patrick.
Frantz Fanon: a spiritual biography / by Patrick Ehlen.
p. cm. – (Lives & Legacies)
Includes bibliographical references and index.
ISBN 0-8245-2354-7
1. Fanon, Frantz, 1925–1961. 2. Fanon, Frantz,
1925–1961—Political and social views.
3. Blacks—Social conditions. 4. Racism. I. Title.
CT2628.F35 E39 2000
322.4'2'092–dc21
[B]   00-009760

Printed in the United States of America
Set in Janson
Designed and produced by SCRIBES Editorial
Cover design by Kaeser and Wilson Design Ltd.

1 2 3 4 5 6 7 8 9 10 04 03 02 01 00

for Gramma Deena,
and in memory of Chick Pallesen

CONTENTS

Frantz Fanon

Frantz Fanon
(Seuil/Olivier Fanon)

1

Je Suis . . .

> O my body,
> make of me always a man who questions!
> —*Frantz Fanon*

I AM A BLACK MAN. I AM A WHITE MAN. I am a Frenchman, a Martinican, an Algerian. I am a hero to my country and I am a traitor to my country. I am the idol of the film, but I am the villain of the film. Am I handsome? Yes, of course; but I am ugly. I am darker than my brother and lighter than my father. I am larger than the universe. I sing, I weep, I dance. I am all men, and no man. I am Frantz. I am Frantz Fanon.

But who am I?

The years since his death offer countless responses: He was a revolutionary, a psychiatrist, a humanist, an existentialist, a Marxist, a nihilist, an anticolonialist, an internationalist, a prophet, a demon, a pope. But in life he subscribed to no ism, would carry the card of no party. From a historical perspective he appeared to make choices based on a single question: Will this choice free souls from their chains? Or better, will this step move humanity toward greater liberation? His answers led him to war with the Nazis, to struggle with himself, to labor against mental illness, and to a bloody and painful revolt against French colonialism in Algeria.

Looking across his life, one sees that he failed at many things. But the luminescence of his successes outshine all loss. In the course of ten years he produced three books, *Black Skin, White Masks*, *A Dying Colonialism*, and *The Wretched of the Earth*, as well as the handful of essays collected in the posthumous collection *Towards the African Revolution*, all of which continue to be read and studied today, perhaps more widely with each passing year. In the United States these works greatly inspired thinkers and activists of the American civil rights movement and the Black Panthers, and offer profound insight on our collective understanding of race, of alienation, and of power and oppression. Some ideas precede those of his generation by several decades and speak plainly to our contemporary dilemma of how we can manage the friction of a world that is increasingly interwoven, fractured and complicated. He wrote for several journals and newspapers, produced three plays, and published a handful of psychiatric studies, consistently pursuing the theme of personal liberation in the face of an alienating society.

Whatever contradictions may be found in the pages of his writings, at no point does he deviate from one premise: that the human mind, the human spirit, and human society are inextricably connected, and that one of these elements cannot be liberated if the others remain in bondage. Even toward the end of his life, when he fought for the seemingly contradictory interests of a single nation's autonomy in hope of achieving a united Africa that would transgress all nationalism, this premise held at the fore. Liberate the individual, grant autonomy to each spirit, and unity will follow—the spirits will merge together. For unity is the natural state of the human spirit, when freed from all chains.

There seems to have been rarely a day that he did not commit to a struggle for freedom. Yet he lived as anyone, managing to fashion from common leaves the wings of a transcendent life, a life devoted to others. Overshadowed by such a figure we are compelled to ask, how was it managed? What condition, what essence, made it possible? To maintain such altitude, when we are all of us pulled down by the cumbersome world . . . But the flight of any grand spirit is achieved through the unsteady flappings of an individual. And the story of Frantz Fanon is the story of a family, the story of an island, and the story of disappointment and loss. And as with many such stories, it is the story of love and tragedy.

For now, let it merely be said that an oppressive society breeds oppression among each person it dominates. Most often this oppression, this fury, is kept within the confines of family relations, or is turned inwards to affect the individual in a self-destructive manner. But sometimes this oppression plants the seed of its own destruction. Sometimes the interior pressure of that force within a single individual reaches an intensity that drives the individual to uncommon lengths, the force recoiling and erupting back outward again, and oppression forges the means of its own undoing. The lesson of history tells us that this is the moment we will witness the spiritual.

It is at this moment—at the moment when a limit is reached and all boundaries give way to an infinitude of possibility—that mundane and material dictums evaporate to reveal the nature of that which crosses every culture and every era, the immutable force of the human spirit. It is a moment of beauty for all who bear it witness, but let us not forget that a beautiful individual is sacrificed in the process. It is at this moment that we witness Gandhi, that we witness Mohammed, that we witness Christ. It is at this moment that we witness Frantz Fanon.

Frantz Fanon's passport photo.
(Algerian National Press and Information Documentation Center)

2

Morne Noire

It is the land of anger, an exasperated land,
a land which spits and spews, which spews life.
That is what we must be worthy of.

—Aimé Césaire

DRY RAIN FELL IN THE CLOSE OF APRIL. Above the island city a vast shadow gathered, a mass of dark cloud spreading along the tropic hills and moving across the Caribbean waters. On the city streets and on the decks of ships in the harbor a pale dust collected, and rancid mud bubbled up in the river that ran through the center of town. At unannounced moments the city floor trembled, and a telegraph cable snapped skyward once when the earth abruptly quivered. In canals that spanned the city the water had long tasted of sulphur, but now the air throughout was foul with the stench. Eyes looked north to the crest of the great mountain that sheltered the city, where jets of vapor escaped from fissures at the peak.

The governor, Louis Mouttet, a French colonist who had lived on Martinique for many years, assured the residents of Saint Pierre that there was nothing to fear, and that the mountain posed no threat to the island's grandest city. To reassure them further he brought his family north from the lesser capital of Fort-de-France and took up temporary residence at a hotel in Saint Pierre. The clouds, the tremors, and the falling ash and pebbles he scientifically explained as a "temporary disturbance" of the kind that occasionally follows the vernal equinox. But as the ground trembled with a more restless ardor and a murky pillar of vapor accumulated above the peak of Mont Pelée, faith in the governor's words began to wane. The cracks and gasps of distant detonations could be heard through half the island. On the fifth day of May, a Monday, an abrupt torrent of mud and water came gushing down a gorge in the mountainside, hailing from a once-tranquil lake at the mountain's crest, and demolished a sugar mill and thirty people along the way. By Wednesday a unanimous consensus was heard among the inhabitants of Saint Pierre that evacuation was a prudent if not compelling idea. The governor spoke again, this time beseeching his constituents to remain until Sunday—the day he had likely held out for all along, so as not to postpone the election polls scheduled that afternoon (polls for which incumbent officials had undoubtedly done a great deal of "preparation," as often accompanied the rigged elections of French colonies in the Third Republic). The people of Saint Pierre conceded. They would go to the polls on Sunday, and then proceed with evacuation. As the dim of night drew over the island, still the sky rained steadily down.

Thursday morning dawned warm and clear, the sun rising behind the forested ridge to redden the western shore below the city's colonial ramparts. To the northern horizon loomed the height of the mountain, its peak enshrined in a vaporous mantle that stretched as high as the drifting clouds. On Thursdays the newspaper was closed and the merchants slept late. The city lay tranquil under tin and copper roofs that sheltered houses of stone and brick, and the odd pedestrian strolled along the bridge that crossed the river to the pioneer fort and resplendent chapel at the center of town. Servants emerged early on the winding cat-paths with jugs to be dumped in the deep gutters that coursed from the hills to the bay. The placid murmur of these canals was the most notable sound, until just after eight when out of the hills a plangent roar ripped into the quiet and a convulsion of netherly smoke burst from the southwestern face of the mountain and plunged down upon the city and out across the sea, its entrails delivering a tempest of gas and ash and stone and a darkness more pitch than the blackest night. The sea itself gave a violent shudder, and islands near and afar beheld a monolithic column of molten rock and cinder that left the summit of Mont Pelée to thrust a mile into the blue heavens. When at last the darkness lifted Saint Pierre was gone, a scarlet glow of embers smoldering where it had stood, and the buildings, the ships in the harbor, and all 30,000 residents of the city had been incinerated in a merciless instant.

In the following days a lone survivor would surface from the ruins, one Auguste Cyparis—known around Saint Pierre as a wastrel drunkard before the eve of the disaster, when his disorderly conduct landed him in a jail dug far beneath the city. This twist of fortune spun him to stardom, and he soon launched a gainful career with P.T. Barnum's circus, presenting his scarred aspect before audiences as the world's greatest "volcano survivor." But Cyparis' fortune was not the only one altered by the tragic eruption, which transformed both the geography and the economy of the island. With the destruction of Saint Pierre the French Antilles lost its largest commercial center; a great majority of the colony's physicians, lawyers, merchants, civil servants, and schoolteachers were now gone—and most had been white French colonists who, as the island's most powerful minority, were already few in number. Now where would the islanders go for these services? And who would now fill these positions? The answer to the first question was Fort-de-France, the hurricane-ravaged port to the south that became the new center of commercial activity in Martinique. The answer to the second question was the black residents of the island, most of whom had been freed from slavery only fifty years before, yet still served as underpaid laborers on sugar plantations or as servants for the colonial landowners, despite their increasing advancement in literacy and education.

And so altered was the fortune of young Casimir Fanon, eleven years old and living behind a sugar mill in the town of Trinité with his father, a freed slave, and his mother, an East Indian, when the ground trembled beneath his feet and he bore witness to the eruption of Mont Pelée on the northern horizon. And when the lifting cloud of ash cleared a view of the mountain base it revealed a gash where colossal pressure within the volcano's obstructed hearth had ruptured its side in the exact direction of Saint Pierre, as though from an ulcer of some infernal origin. The mountain erupted twice again that summer, engulfing another town in the heat of late August, and the towering dome of ash and rock did not retreat to the mountain's cone until July of the following year.

In the years of economic reconstruction that followed, Casimir educated himself enough to secure a government position in Fort-de-France, and there he met a young and beautiful mulatto from the town of Vauclin named Eléonore Médélice. Eléonore's family had traveled to Martinique from Alsace, a region of dispute between France and Germany until France claimed its title at Versailles. While Martinicans would call Eléonore an *enfant reconnue*—a daughter of unmarried parents— the legitimacy of her birth was not nearly as essential to her social standing as the fact of her Alsatian background and the fairness of her skin. For the interests of Casimir, these details would present a small challenge.

An understanding of the challenge before him first invites a look at the social condition of Martinique, and at one of the devastating effects of French colonialism on the island. For Martinique was an island that had suffered great psychic turmoil under the custody of colonial rule, an island subjected to a collective neurosis not unlike that found in a solitary and unwanted stepchild, adopted by the motherland yet kept at a distance and tended with a cool hand, and concurrently accepted in speech while rejected in sentiment and action. It was an island that, in the interest of mercantilism and imperial expansion spanning three centuries, had cast together the complex and varied cultural backgrounds of Europeans, Africans, East Indians, Chinese, and other nationalities, hosting one of the most culturally diverse populations of its time. Yet with nearly 160,000 such inhabitants remaining after the destruction of Saint Pierre in 1902, it also was an island with hardly a thousand white European colonists—or *békés*—who remained socially isolated from the population at large, while maintaining oversight of the impoverished labor class and an emerging middle class through the narcotic of alcohol and through social prohibitions that served a single purpose: to keep the land and commerce in the hands of the outnumbered colonials.

As a result, Martinique became an island where a growing, unstable, and uncertain black middle class were coerced into embracing a racist prejudice as its own measuring stick for social status. And, as too often occurs among populations that endure generations of oppression, it became an island whose restrained hostility toward its oppressors now focused inwards to target those aspects of itself that recalled its memory of enslavement. The estranged stepchild would surmise its own worth by comparison to those who were accepted without question. Social privileges issued from prejudicial standards: skin tone, facial characteristics, and speech often determined a person's fortune. Furthering the social and economic advancement of one's children became a question of making oneself as close to the *békés* in all outward appearance—or, as Frantz Fanon would later characterize it, the "most white"—as one could possibly become.

Such was the cultural tide that flowed against the romantic exertions of Casimir, son of a former slave and wholly working-class, and by no means of the caste that the parents of the fair and beautiful Eléonore had aspired to bequeath their daughter. Still, Casimir was a charming and intelligent freethinker, in many ways a self-made man, and to his further fortune Eléonore was not a woman to let the prejudices of her parents' society stand in the way of something she wanted. Soon they were married, and lived happily and comfortably on the outskirts of Fort-de-France. By 1925 she had given birth to two daughters and two sons—Mireille, Félix, Gabrielle, and Joby—and on the twentieth day of July in that year she found herself blessed with another son, whom she named Frantz. While the other children were comparably fair in complexion and their appearance reflected the French heritage of their mother, Frantz more resembled his father, with distinctly dark skin and strong African features. These differences coupled with Frantz's early willfulness prompted his parents to joke that perhaps the baby had been switched at the hospital, but they soon remarked other differences in this new child, who spoke and walked at an early age and revealed an indefatigable energy and fascination with the world.

In the course of another eight years two more daughters and one son would complete the Fanon family—Marie-Flore, Laurette and Willy. In 1929, when Frantz was only four, the ground again trembled and Casimir again looked north with a nervous eye directed toward Pelée, concealing his fear before the children while the mountain hiccuped and an ashen cloud deprived Fort-de-France of sun for nearly a week. A similar incident would occur again three years later, as if to remind the residents of Martinique that the very earth on which they worked and lived existed by virtue of a supreme and incomprehensible violence.

Though Casimir worked hard as a customs inspector and the Fanons never suffered from great economic discomfort, their financial condition kept them at close quarters. As a result the family was close-knit, and the children got along as well as one could expect. As a mother, Eléonore made an extraordinary effort to foster a sense of unity within the family, especially in times of hardship, and she would often exhort, "My children, it's *unity*—and *unity alone*—that saves the family, and each one of us. As long as you are united, you are strong. That which belongs to one of us belongs to everyone, and thereby we are all rich." In enforcing this maxim of unity she was adamant. It was the most critical ethic she sought to teach her family, and Madame Fanon strictly reinforced the principle in the minds of her children by repeated and unbending example.

From time to time Casimir's brother came to Fort-de-France to settle business and to visit the family, and the children eagerly anticipated the arrival of Uncle Albert, who never failed to produce for them some extra change from his pocket. On one July day when Frantz was five or six, Uncle Albert had become particularly generous just as the ice-cream man approached, and after much excitement and indecision over what flavor each child wanted most, they at last settled themselves in the shade of the verandah with their treats and enjoyed a cool and sweet recess to a hot afternoon. Shortly after the ice-cream man had gone, Madame Fanon emerged to sit among her children, finding their faces soiled with gluttonous satisfaction. Leaning over to Frantz's sister Gabrielle, she implored, "Let me have a taste."

Gabrielle, eating slowly but wanting not to lose one drop, looked to her mother in complaint and demanded, "Why me?" At this and without further ado Madame Fanon sprung to her feet, plucked the cone from her daughter's hands, and flung it against a tree in the yard. Gabrielle watched in tearful horror as her cherished ice cream slumped down the trunk of the tree, and the children sat astonished, trembling with frozen gazes before their mother as she thundered, "What belongs to me belongs to you. What belongs to you belongs to all of us. Put that into your head, once and for all!"

It was a lesson not one child would forget.

Martinique did not go untouched by economic depression in the 1930s, and when the family income was pinched Madame Fanon compensated by adding a small business to her already busy schedule of mothering eight children. The downstairs drawing room of their house then opened to the public as a small boutique, where passersby could purchase any manner of items that Madame Fanon conceived to sell with her keen sense of enterprise. When the family's economic condition slowly improved, they were able to move further downtown, and to afford homes that were slightly more accommodating for a family of ten. As they exchanged residences for homes that came closer and closer to the center of Fort-de-France—where the sprawling palm-lined park of the *Savane* met weary world travelers off the bay with shops and cafés and cinemas and taverns—there swelled a sentiment among the children that the family was climbing higher on the social ladder; and when at last they moved into a spacious home two blocks from the *Savane* and right at the heart of the action, the exhilaration among the children reflected a sense that they had finally reached the very top.

This sense of achievement was paralleled in the unspoken

Houses overlooking Fort-de-France.
(Photo by author)

Fountain
at town center,
Fort-de-France.
(Photo by author)

Breton Encounters Négritude

In the spring of 1941 a group of dissident artists and intellectuals—among them French poet André Breton and painter André Masson, as well as Cuban painter Wilfredo Lam—fled Nazi-occupied France for the French Antilles, only to meet an unwelcoming arrival on landing a month later in Fort-de-France.

Hoping to escape persecution or incarceration under Nazi rule in Paris, they arrived to find the tropical sanctuary they had envisioned was dominated by Vichyist Admiral Robert, and the ship's passengers were promptly arrested and confined to a former leper colony at Lazeret.

André Breton eventually managed to escape their captivity for a few days, and promptly began exploring the streets of Fort-de-France for what Paul Éluard had described to him as "women more beautiful than anywhere else."

In search of a ribbon to bring back to his daughter, Breton entered a shop owned by the sister of poet René Ménil, where the journal Ménil helped to produce, *Tropiques*, was displayed in the window. Deprived of intellectual nourishment for some time, Breton opened the journal and read the words of Césaire. He later wrote:

"I could not believe my eyes: But what was said there, it was what had to be said—and not only in the best manner, but as strong as one could possibly say it! All of these grimacing shades tore apart, dispersed; all of these lies, all of these derisions fell in rags: so the man's voice was in no way broken, covered; it here righted itself as a stalk does to light. *Aimé Césaire*: that was the name of the voice who spoke."

Though previously discouraged by the pretense of pre-war French poetry, this fresh voice brought hope for the future of literature to Breton, and his search for women was forgotten in favor of a search for this new and brilliant sculptor of words.

Breton soon befriended Césaire—as did Wilfredo Lam—and counseled Césaire on the tracts of surrealism, encouraging him to more daring heights in the acrobatics of language. When Breton returned to France in 1943, he republished Césaire's poem *Cahier d'un Retour au Pays Natal*, and helped to champion the recognition of *négritude* as a major literary movement.

fancies of Casimir, also drawn to the magnetic vitality of the city. But then, who could not be so drawn? At the heart of Fort-de-France the rising bourgeoisie could find escape from its toils and reward for its ambitions. Here they found fashionable social circles that flaunted colorful garments as they strolled the *Savane* and retreated to parlors to dance the *béguine*. Here they found rum in endless reserve, cheap and amply supplied by the *békés*, and taverns that served until dawn. Here men gathered in circles around once and returning travelers to be beguiled with tales of Paris and its jazz clubs and its shimmering madness. And here Casimir would find men of like-minded sentiments, critical of the old guard but uncertain of its alternatives, and could pass the evening in good-humored debate.

Such men of island society spent long hours with one another and little time elsewhere, and their families could go days without sight of them. Casimir Fanon was not a glowing exception to the practice, though his wife was an exception in her refusal to accept it, and made every effort to persuade him also to comply with her dictum of family unity. In exasperation at some failed attempts to do so, she one day sent the children out to post an announcement where they knew Monsieur Fanon would not miss it. The announcement read, "Urgent! A handsome prize shall go to anyone who sees or apprehends a father with eight children!" Shortly thereafter, when Monsieur Fanon walked through the door and asked for his handsome prize, he was rewarded with a smile from Madame Fanon and the teasing reply, "You got the prize already—since there can be no more handsome prize than the love of eight children, and of their mother!"

Like most families in Martinique, the Fanons baptized their children as Catholic, encouraging modern Catholic values in the home and appearing regularly at church on Sundays. The frequent absentee among them was Monsieur Fanon, whose spiritual interests found greater fulfillment among the Freemasons, and who led a fairly liberal, though not dispassionate, spiritual life. In a curious way, little Frantz's inner life would later evolve to most resemble that of his father. By the time he was old enough to choose his own mode of spiritual expression, Frantz had moved away from his traditional Catholic upbringing in favor of a more modern, existentialist faith, rooted in an ethic of personal responsibility. The papal saints of his childhood—who each received a day of fervent celebration on Martinique—would be supplanted for Frantz by those saints of the modern intellect who extolled the preeminence of individual choice. Though Frantz would not turn to Kierkegaard, Nietzsche, Jaspers, and Sartre (who later befriended him) until further in his education, even his earliest years revealed an ardent and almost pious respect for the sanctity of action. And it is interesting to note that, in view of Monsieur Fanon's devotion to a rather passive and sanctimonious spirituality of talk, Frantz would come to develop an acute skepticism of and disdain for mere speech, and, as his view of his own station in the world matured, he became ever more firmly devoted to the primacy of action.

Speech itself occupied a sacred space for Frantz from an early age, and its sacredness was ingrained not only within his family but throughout the surrounding culture. Here the subtle quality of one's speech—whether it resembled the choppy patois of the Creole dialect heard among the lower classes, or more the stiff, over-enunciated and formal French uttered by the upper classes and the *béké* colonists—served to tie the single most binding knot to one's social and economic standing, invoking more social discrimination than even the inveterate racism woven throughout the island. A man who spoke proper French, "the

French of France," could bargain for a certain degree of respect in his interactions; but the speaker of island Creole could expect no such bargain. Fanon later observed that the colonized individual "is elevated above his jungle status in proportion to his adoption of the mother country's cultural standards." For the colonies of France, and no less for Martinique, that standard was foremost determined by language.

In the true spirit of French colonialism, Martinique was dominated culturally as much as it was economically, burying local history and culture beneath the values of the French mainland, consistent with France's "assimilationist" policy toward its colonies. In the name of assimilation, France sought to persuade its colonial subjects that they were not merely subjects of France, but rather that they *were* French—complete with a mirage of equality that helped to pacify resistance against colonization and to supplant any rebellious energies with a kind of cultural rivalry, amounting at bottom to disputes over those qualities that made any one person "more French" than the next. Hence the first words little Frantz learned to write in school were *"Je suis français."* He and his classmates, most of whom were grandchildren of African slaves, listened to lessons about "our ancestors, the Gauls." On the walls of the classroom he studied maps of Bordeaux and the Savoie and learned about the economy of the wine harvest, but learned next to nothing about the Caribbean islands or the brutal history of the slave trade or the sugar fields only a few miles away, where the majority of men in Martinique still toiled to make a living.

As with most middle-class families who aspired to higher social positions on the island, the Fanons were quite conscious of the impact of outward appearances on their social standing. Creole was never spoken, except to servants and persons considered of lower class, and when Frantz or the other children slipped into slang they could expect to be chastised by Madame Fanon, who would drop her voice in disapproval and say, "Don't behave like a nigger." Madame Fanon encouraged the use of proper, if not impeccable, French, and the children would grow up to exhibit a solid command of the French language—the so-called "French of France" that out measured all but the rarest Frenchman in its correctness. But the most conspicuous among them in his cultivation of verbal command was Frantz, who over the years would transform Madame Fanon's insistence on rigid grammatical propriety into an extraordinary and uncannily superior facility with language—an aspect of Frantz's persona that would strike most anyone he met throughout his lifetime, from teachers to his latest acquaintances. The solemn respect for language with which he spoke and wrote never seemed to falter.

On most counts Frantz was a typical child, given the culture he grew up in. As the second youngest of four boys he was fiercely competitive, and struggled mightily to prove himself among his older brothers and their friends. The curious result of this struggle was that he would spend many of his growing years around children who were slightly older than he was, and who would all soon look to him as the deviser of solutions and the instigator of escapades. He was mischievous and irreverent both in and out of school, and rarely wasted a moment between contriving a plan for some scheme and enlisting a crew of followers to help him carry it out. He exhibited the average boy's less-than-angelic patience for the tedium of school or church, and at such times often resorted to making up his own entertainments. On one occasion in church he produced a box of pins and engaged the clandestine efforts of other children to assist him in pinning together the dresses of women around them. The operation was difficult and perilous, and required utmost dexterity and stealth as the children held straight faces and pretended to contemplate the sermon while they worked. But their efforts paid off when at last the women rose to receive communion, attempting to reach the sanctuary by various directions but instead finding themselves tied from both ends by the tether among their skirts, and as the women looked at one another in baffled consternation the children exploded into riotous laughter. Though Frantz remained cool and appeared as confounded as his mother, Madame Fanon maintained her suspicions of who had instigated the entire ordeal.

Indeed, Frantz was considered a regular troublemaker both by his parents and sisters at home and by his teachers and classmates in school. But his mischief proactively aided in hiding a deep sensitivity, as he was easily offended or hurt, and often guarded and unforgiving when he felt he had been wronged. He was precociously empathetic when dealing with other children, and felt deeply betrayed when they did not afford him a similar consideration. In compensation, he could affect an intentionally aggressive style if he wanted to be taken seriously. He rebuffed out of hand any suggestions of compromise or rule-bending while playing at soccer or other games, and he exhibited a particular deliberateness in his demeanor and his actions that at times bordered on strict rigidity. A paradox of Frantz's personality—at bottom not so puzzling—was his strict observance of those rules that protected his sense of autonomy and coherence, while displaying a rebellious and mocking disdain for any rule or symbol of authority that failed to contribute to that conception. His unfailing attention to authority and disposition of strictness regarding his personal outlook would accompany him throughout his life, and would become well-known but rarely-discussed aspects of Frantz's personality for anyone who knew him. Moreover, these traits invariably came into play when he made assessments of others or of himself, and resulted in a purposeful, attentive and collected demeanor.

As early as the age of eight, young Frantz exhibited a cool composure that rivaled even the friends of his fourteen-year-old brother Félix. One friend of Félix's was a boy named Kléber, who could be found at the Fanon household with a frequency that nearly earned him status as a fifth brother in the Fanon family. Kléber, however, was slightly less scrupulous than the others. This want of scruple led him one afternoon to appear at the Fanon house with his father's revolver tucked beneath his shirt, anticipating that Félix would be duly impressed. When Madame Fanon told him Félix had gone out on an errand, Kléber wandered upstairs to wait in the boys' room, now occupied only by young Frantz. Eager to show the revolver to someone, Kléber was soon displaying it to Frantz, boasting of his knowledge and skill with the gun. To add some sophistication to his demonstration, he took off the safety, polished the gun a little, and clicked the trigger.

He had presumed the revolver was not loaded.

A shot rang out, and the bullet missed Frantz by mere inches. The boys exchanged astonished glances, and then looked at the gun in Kléber's hand. The gun and the hand were covered in blood. One of Kléber's fingers was torn by the bullet. Madame Fanon yelled upstairs to inquire about the noise. With reserved composure Frantz replied that a toy had backfired, while quietly ripping his bed sheet to bandage Kléber's finger. Minutes later Frantz casually announced that he and Kléber were going out for a walk, and the two boys rushed off to the hospital in town.

Kléber was not surprised by Frantz's efficiency; in fact, it was just what he knew to expect, for Frantz exhibited such impenetrable poise in every game he played and, indeed, in everything he did. His determined composure in the face of trouble would one day contribute crucially to the struggles and achievements of his life.

But those purposes to which he would later dedicate his undaunted nature had yet to concern him. Racism, colonialism, psychology, and politics—these things were still far from overtly significant in the consciousness of Frantz, or for his brothers and friends, who for now played and cavorted with a kind of benighted exhilaration. At the cinema they watched French and American films and superimposed themselves on the images of exalted Western conquerors and heroes. The cinematic villains of their nightmares they recognized in images of black "natives" like the Senegalese—those barbaric African warriors who pillaged jungle terrains, cutting off heads and collecting human ears. And when they played around the *Savane* on humid afternoons under the marbled guard of Empress Josephine, they played cowboys shooting brutal Indians or explorers slaying savage headhunters. And when they boasted of achievements to come, they boasted of journeys to France, the great motherland, in whose name they were sure to accomplish the grandest adventures. And at night when they lay down their heads and dreamed, they dreamed the fair dreams of their colonizers.

The dream would continue until 1939.

Aimé Césaire
(© Bettmann/CORBIS)

3

War from Within, War from Without

Know it well:
I never play if not at the millennium
I never play if not at the Great Fear.

Get used to me. I will not get used to you!
—*Aimé Césaire*

FIFTEEN YEARS AFTER THE FACT, Frantz Fanon would count three successive events that changed the face of Martinique after 1939. The first event was the return from Europe of the young poet and intellectual Aimé Césaire, who began teaching the youth of Fort-de-France at the *lycée Schoelcher.* The second event was the outbreak of war in France, the subsequent vanquishment of the motherland that devastated the residents of Martinique, and the occupation of the island by soldiers of the Vichy regime. And the third event was the awakening of Martinicans to a political and racial consciousness that would allow the island to recognize itself as a political entity with interests and concerns distinct from those of Europe. But looking at Frantz as a boy in his teens, and looking at those objects that made the most immediate, personal and lasting impression on his young mind, these events can easily be narrowed down to representation by a single name, and that name was Césaire.

When he began teaching high school at the *lycée* in 1939, twenty-six-year-old Aimé Césaire had recently returned from an eight-year sojourn in Paris, where he attended the distinguished

École Normale Supérieure. Much like the young student Frantz Fanon, Césaire had come from a large middle-class family (his father was a civil servant and his mother a dressmaker) who valued education enough to make sacrifices to pay for him to attend the *lycée*—the only private school on the island that was not exclusively for whites. There his sharp intellect and verbal ability won him prizes in French, Latin, English, and history, and a scholarship to study in Paris. This fact alone would have brought him a respectful reputation when he returned home, for a man educated in Paris was a man who had reached a particular level of perfection in the esteem of the island bourgeoisie, a man who now embodied a certain mythological essence from having moved, thought and spoken in the exalted white world of the motherland.

But Césaire was to secure himself a much different kind of reputation on his return, as he had secured himself a much different kind of education through his associations in Paris. Far from returning to Martinique to carry on the indoctrination of young minds into those prejudiced ideas and values of the mother country, Césaire returned to profess a concept that was wholly radical for the island community; the concept was called *négritude*, and it conveyed in the plainest and most persuasive words the mere statement that it was wonderfully fortunate to be black, and that anyone who aspired to be otherwise did so at the greatest of costs.

His assertions were scandalous, and impossible to ignore when they pierced the psychological core of even the most unwilling listener. Césaire had challenged the fundamental and implicit drive among every Martinican to identify with the aggressor and to accept without question the motherland's bid for assimilation. Consider, then, the impact of such notions on a young black student who had only years before penned an essay about summer vacation with the words, "I can run through the fields, breathe fresh air, and come home with rosy cheeks." Or consider the ruminations that must occur to a boy who would time and again hear his mother say plainly of him, "Oh, he is the blackest of my children"—and sense that in these words she revealed the whole of what society viewed as most flawed in his very being.

Césaire exerted an astounding influence on many young intellects of Martinique, and especially on the *lycée* student Frantz Fanon. But it must be noted that few persons of the time were open to that influence, and were, perhaps, looking to be so influenced. That is to propose that Frantz's influence by Césaire was in some ways primed by the influence of an earlier relationship, the relationship with his older brother Joby.

As the next oldest brother and only two years ahead of Frantz, Joby was Frantz's closest childhood companion. All of the brothers were close, constantly running together in sports and games, and shared many of the same friends. Félix exhibited much of Frantz's audacity and tendency toward trouble, but Joby offered Frantz a deeper side that appealed to Frantz's inclination toward profundity. Quieter and stockier than Frantz but equally disposed to laughs and a good prank, he balanced Frantz's daring spirit with an older brother's temperament of responsibility and guidance. While Frantz permitted himself hardly a moment to move from the conception of an idea to its execution, it was Joby who stepped in as the voice of forethought and consideration, careful to point out options and consequences of an otherwise precipitous action. Joby may have felt powerless when it came to influencing Frantz's decisions, and also rather timorous in comparison to the bravado shown by his younger brother, but in many ways he played the role of a safety net that heightened Frantz's confidence as Frantz traversed wires that rose higher with the passing of each year, and Joby's solicitous guardianship allowed his little brother to move from impulses that would otherwise have been too dangerous to mobilize.

In their early teens the boys and some neighborhood friends had formed a tight enough group to regard their circle as a small gang, calling themselves *la Bande Raide* ("the Stiff Gang"), and counted among their members several rascals with nicknames like *"Kabere"* (Frantz), *"Pipo"* (Joby), *"Belle Tête"* and *"Gros Lombric."* Allowing not the least conformist among them, the *Bande Raide* engaged in youthful antics that mostly aspired to upset the respectable society represented by their mothers and sisters. Their exploits were not limited to sneaking into the cinema without paying, and stealing billiard balls and small items from local boutiques, beginning with that of Madame Fanon. A singular rule of the gang called for no leader among them save he who had conceived the latest escapade and dared to direct the others toward execution of the plan. Of course this rule frequently put Frantz, with his reverence for action, at the head of the gang, and Joby directly at his heels, apprehensive in his sense of responsibility as the older brother and knowing he would be held responsible if news of their mischief reached his mother's ears.

Much of the time it did, and though Madame Fanon was perfectly aware of Frantz's indomitable leadership among his peers, she also had a keen awareness of the stalwart bond between her two sons, and of the symbiotic relationship by which the two boys fed from each other and spurred each other into situations that neither were likely to take on alone. Respectful of this bond between them, she was nevertheless challenged to find ways to keep the two out of trouble, which did not preclude evenings when she hid their clothing and shoes, and then proceeded to make them wear the dresses of their sisters. The boys were then free to go where they wished, but her tactic was reliably effective in keeping them at a fair distance from the *Bande Raide* for the night.

If ever there was a time that a family needed the kind of unity Madame Fanon strove for, the time would be 1939—a year that divided families as swiftly as it divided nations. In Europe the merciless warmongering of Hitler's Germany had taken Czechoslovakia and then Poland, and by the second weekend of September France and Britain had issued a declaration of war and were in the throes of fierce combat with German military forces. Though Martinique was far from the struggle of the motherland, the German military spanned enough of the globe that bombings of Fort-de-France became a fear throughout the city. Classes at the *lycée* were canceled, and summer vacation extended by default. Radios in all corners of the city brought the war into every home and tavern. Accounts from the streets gorged the imaginations of the *Bande Raide*, and the grassy *Savane* became their smoldering battlefield, its trenches lined with brave young heroes.

But more free time brought more trouble for the boys, and also for their mother. By November Madame Fanon felt overwhelmed enough to send Joby across the island to live with his Uncle Edouard in the town of François. Frantz had many close friends in the city, but with Joby suddenly gone he grew uncommonly quiet and withdrawn. In an act of barely subtle protest, he left the house early in the morning and returned only for meals, ate with sullen reserve, and then went out again without a word. This situation continued for several days. Then one afternoon at the lunch table, as Frantz ate silently among the family, Monsieur Fanon at last inquired about the whereabouts of his absent son. Joby had gone to François, Madame Fanon casually answered, for his classes. It was a thin story, and Casimir did not buy it for a minute. With a note of reprimand he instructed his wife to have Joby returned to Fort-de-France at once, and furthermore never again to make arrangements for his children without his permission. Madame Fanon glared at him across the table. The children looked on. Then in an impenetrable tone she announced, "Not only will Joby not return to Fort-de-France, but Frantz leaves today for François to stay with his uncle."

Monsieur Fanon recoiled slightly, inspecting his wife. He then made his best effort to recover. "I require that on my return from the office this evening my sons will be *here*," he said. "Otherwise, we shall see!"

Madame Fanon replied, "There is nothing to see; you can count on it. Tonight there will be no Joby, no Frantz. If you want to see them, you will be going to retrieve them in François."

For nearly a year from this day the two boys lived with Uncle Edouard, a confirmed bachelor who nonetheless regarded Joby and Frantz as his own sons. Edouard reveled in providing them the education they were otherwise missing, and in their uncle the boys found a positive male role model they had heretofore lacked in the frequently absent and remote figure of their father. A devoted reader and thinker, Edouard ignited the interests of his nephews in moral philosophy and in the classics of French literature, and he encouraged them to challenge their thinking in ways that diverged from the uninspired lecturing they had thus far received in school. It was a pivotal period in the development of both boys. Unlike what they had grown accustomed to at home, Uncle Edouard held them to no strict rules or autocratic regimens, and all decision making was achieved by democratic consensus. As a result, the tremendous energies these young men had formerly dedicated to rebellions against their parents and petit-bourgeois society were now free to be redirected toward more productive efforts. They read, thought, debated and discussed. Politics surrounding the war provided a daily forum for moral reflection, and their previously undirected attentions found new and exciting points of focus. In more ways than one, they were growing up.

May 10, 1940: The Nazis invade France, taking the border region of Alsace with the force of brutal lightning. The losing struggle on the motherland is intensely felt on Martinique, and the seizure of Madame Fanon's birthplace is particularly painful for the Fanon family. Far worse lay ahead. June brought news of German bombs tearing down upon their beloved Paris, and within three weeks Nazis marched through the Arc de Triomphe, Marshal Pétain became the French Prime Minister and installed the Nazi-friendly Vichy government, and Hitler stood beneath the Eiffel Tower to survey the prize of his bold and sinister efforts.

For the inhabitants of Martinique, news of the fall of France to Germany can only be likened to news of the death of a parent—the only parent the island had ever known. It was a humiliating defeat, even at this remote location, and Frantz vehemently shared the indignation and fury of young men on Martinique at the aggressive injustice that symbolically assailed their ascension to manhood. Frantz was perhaps all the more indignant, given the moral education he had so recently been exposed to in his uncle's care. Soon these feelings would multiply tenfold, as the war affronted the tranquil sensibilities of the islanders in a far more intimate manner.

The coming to power of the Vichy regime readily gained the allegiance of a disturbing number of French military leaders, including Admiral Georges Robert, who commanded the French naval fleet in the Caribbean. Thanks to influence from Berlin, the reward for such allegiance was a prolonged vacation that would keep French naval forces out of the way of Nazi operations, and the French Caribbean navy was granted an indefinite shore leave. As a result, in the summer of 1940 some 5,000 French sailors disembarked at Fort-de-France, and, after summoning their wives and families from the mainland, effectively increased the number of white Europeans on the island from two thousand to nearly five times that number.

Martinique was ill-equipped to deal with the strain on its resources that accompanied these additional mouths to feed and bodies to house, especially after British blockades cut off trade with Europe. Even more troublesome than these economic stresses were the psychological stresses that accompanied the forced reorganization of a once well-stratified society. For although the sinuous threads of racial discrimination had long been woven into the social fabric that enveloped the island's population, these threads had become so tightly knit as to appear effectively invisible to most people. The small ruling class of *békés* had remained sequestered from the larger population, and blatant acts of racism were uncommon. Though Fort-de-France had provided temporary accommodation to shore parties of French sailors in the past, the parties were few in number and brief in the duration of their stay, and conflicts were limited and isolated. Then, in the course of a few weeks, thousands of discontented French outsiders disembarked upon the island, arriving with no knowledge of or concern for its cultural precedents, and they at once commenced to tearing through the shroud of equanimity that had formerly existed, confronting the island's black citizens with flagrant and unmitigated racism.

Fort-de-France's picturesque landscape was transformed overnight. The military used its authority to requisition everything from hotels to whorehouses, and every public facility became segregated and downright inhospitable to its former patrons. Racist slurs and violent threats multiplied with each day.

The proud members of Martinique's petit-bourgeois class, who through their social achievements had heretofore made every effort to convince themselves that they were now as culturally distinct from labor-class blacks as any European, found themselves continually humiliated by these ignorant and brutish intruders who viewed them in the manner they most despised to be viewed: as insignificant, second-class citizens. And these psychological abuses paled in comparison to physical abuses the military occupation wrought upon the island. Restless and drunken sailors did not hesitate to assault any islander who challenged or displeased them, and the rape of Martinique's young women became a rampant and neglected tragedy, with police promptly dismissing claims levied by blacks against the white military occupants.

With Fort-de-France facing such unprecedented turmoil, the Fanons did their best to keep their children away from the city, and Joby and Frantz remained with Uncle Edouard through the end of the following summer. But in spite of the drastically deteriorating conditions in Fort-de-France, the new regime had relieved the city of the threat of bombings or other German aggression, and the *lycée* was able to reopen. This fact brought Frantz and Joby back to their parents' home come September, as well as to the city they had once subverted in their escapades but which now lay waiting in menace for the least sign of impertinence among its young residents. The times called for discretion and attentiveness, and the unruly dissidents of the *Bande Raide* no longer had reason to seek benign, conformist adversaries in their mothers and sisters. A real and formidable foe now populated the streets around them.

Climbing the hill to the *lycée* in the morning and descending again in the afternoon, the young men looked down upon the expanse of bay, its bending palms surrounding a fleet of majestic and still warships anchored fast in the harbor. The city spread wide below them. Who were these deplorable intruders? Where had they come from? Were these callous men and women really the "civilized" French heroes they had so long admired, whom they had so long aspired to become? Surely they were not. Surely they were the most despicable and rejected citizens the motherland could offer. But even this explanation offered comfort to no one; the only rationalization that satisfied the disillusioned youth of Martinique—and many of their elders as well—was that the invaders represented the enemy itself, and that owing to their Vichy allegiance the men and women brought by Admiral Robert were no less than Nazis in French clothing, representing a symbolic occupation of Martinique that paralleled and identified directly with the German occupation of the motherland.

This was the position taken adamantly by Frantz, and he came to believe it more strongly with each day that the war carried on. And though many of his would-be rebellions were by necessity transferred to stowage in the realm of his intellect, still his compulsion toward action was at times unassailable. On one early morning before school, Frantz and two of his closest schoolmates, Marcel Manville and Pierre Mosole, were killing time by kicking a ball around the grass of the deserted *Savane*, when across the park they spotted two burly white sailors also kicking at something in the dirt. After stopping to look more closely, they realized the sailors were brutally beating a young Martinican of no more than fifteen who lay helpless on the ground. Though Manville and Mosole were both three years older and larger than Frantz, it was Frantz who without pause went barreling toward the scene and was at grips with the two sailors before his friends could arrive. When the two sailors at last backed off, they explained the youth had pickpocketed one of the men, and they had overcome him as he ran away.

Having recovered the wallet and now finding themselves out-numbered by this unhappy crew of locals, the sailors promptly trod off. The three young men helped the battered youth to his feet and escorted him to the police station to get him some first aid. Later they fell into a discussion, and though they all agreed on the necessity of the intervention to defend a boy from men who would beat someone weaker than themselves, Manville admonished Frantz for not waiting for the three of them to discuss a plan of what they ought to do. Things could have turned out much worse than they did, as the students could have faced arrest for confronting members of the military, or could have been beaten themselves if other sailors had arrived on the scene. But for Frantz, a situation such as this summoned in him something that surpassed all consideration of consequence; it was not possible for him to deliberate, to discuss. The impetuous nature of his boyhood and the moral sensibility he had developed in recent years had now fused into an immediate and unbending sense of duty. He could not allow himself to stand by in idle discussion while another person suffered. Discussion amounted at bottom to fear, and any fear that disallowed or deferred action was intolerable to him. It was weak. It was impotent.

Indeed, the entire island was stricken with a gnawing sense of impotence. The regular inhabitants of Martinique felt degraded and bitter at being cast aside on their own island, and the expatriated sailors became all the more irascible as months and months passed in which they could not return home. In the excruciating course of these three years of naval occupation, two lone voices sounded out in remedy, the voices of Césaire and De Gaulle.

Before the military occupation of the island, Césaire's voice was barely heeded. Most often the teacher was described as "a little mad," and his colleagues at the *lycée* readily offered theories as to what they believed ailed his mental state. For how could a man not be mad who contradicted the common wisdom of generations and proclaimed to the world in public "that it is fine and good to be a Negro," and then augmented this lunacy with the suggestion that when one abandoned one's aspiration toward otherness and embraced the deep interiors of one's authentic being—be it black or otherwise—there existed an ineluctable source of beauty and truth? These assertions indeed seemed delirious, and the surreal turns of phrase in Césaire's seminal long poem, *Cahier d'un Retour au Pays Natal*, did not help to dispel this impression. Fortunately the contents of his book were not widely known, as it had been printed only in Paris in 1939, and the local literary review edited by him and his wife Suzanne, *Tropiques*, devoted to the concept of *négritude*, received limited attention.

But these sentiments were soon to change as circumstances grew more dire. Suddenly confronted with a prevalent racism as they had never known in the past, the residents of Martinique lent a renewed ear to this *lycée* teacher, and his urgings for pride and self-respect among the downtrodden became infinitely more appealing. Aside from his increased recognition around town, Césaire became the most popular teacher at the *lycée*, and among his greatest admirers were Frantz and Joby. Through Césaire's fiery lectures they unearthed and pondered the belligerent songs of forsaken and accursed poets like Baudelaire and Lautréamont. They also discovered modern poets and thinkers crucial to the contentious *négritude* movement, including Césaire's friends Léopold Sédar Senghor of Senegal and Léon-Gontran Damas of Guiana, and Frantz became an avid reader of the journal *Tropiques*.

For Frantz, Césaire's unyielding esteem for individual will and strength of purpose integrated perfectly into his own con-

Students at the lycée Schoelcher.
(Photo by author)

Schoelcher Library
on the Savane
in Fort-de-France.
(Photo by author)

victions of a higher, individual moral authority that transcended the actual and repugnant authorities he was made to endure each day. Beyond this, in Césaire he found a young, well-spoken intellectual from a middle-class family—a man not only of words but of brazen action, who never hesitated to speak his mind regardless of possible consequence or public outcry. Did these qualities not seem familiar to him? And not only had this man earned the gradual respect of their skeptical city, he was also highly admired and praised by André Breton, and had frequented Parisian circles that most Martinicans only read and dreamed about.

An unremarkable and indifferent student up until this point, Frantz suddenly livened under Césaire's influence and began to put his own verbal talents to the test on paper, mostly in flattering imitation of Césaire's style. When Césaire produced plays, Frantz was inspired to take up drama as well, and his animated and charismatic personality proved a perfect fit for this endeavor. He had an impressive presence on the stage and easily slipped into the skins of others. Even when casually telling a story to friends there was a dramatic flare to his demeanor as his face changed from one instant to the next, acting out the parts of people he described.

By default, young women adored Frantz. Not only was he handsome, tall, charismatic, well-spoken, and athletic, but not far below the surface of his conceit one readily uncovered a deeply sensitive side that instinctively sympathized with others. And Frantz in turn adored the women, though he still felt unsure about his own attractiveness. Regardless, he had many girlfriends, and admired many others—including the woman who would soon choose to marry his brother Félix.

The war went on. From the British Caribbean islands radio transmissions brought the voice of General Charles De Gaulle, and with it confirmation for Martinicans that Vichy collaborationists were spineless traitors who had given away their country. De Gaulle became the new bringer of truth. He confirmed that these despicable bearers of the French flag were not in fact French, but something entirely contrary. It now became clear that the racists who filled their streets and cafés represented not the real France, but a fraudulent and corrupted France—for everyone knew that the real French were not racist. For the first time, when patrols of sailors marched down the esplanade of the *Savane* in the evening and called for respect and attention as the *Marseillaise* was played, local men stood by in willful protest and refused to remove their hats, knowing now for certain that this vacantly trumpeted anthem was not *their* anthem, not the anthem of France, but an anthem stolen, sullied and shamed.

The young men of the island became charged with the news of organized resistance, and Frantz was exhilarated by De Gaulle's broadcasts and call to arms. He spoke excitedly about the movement for liberation, and described how De Gaulle's Free French Forces would chase the Germans from France. But how did one join in the fight? In Martinique there were too many armed Vichy soldiers for any movement to prosper. The only possibility was to escape to a more remote location like Dominica, the rainforest-dense island some fifty miles to the north, where one could join the ranks of the real struggle. However, even getting to Dominica was not easy. Fishermen with small boats secretly ferried volunteers at night to the other islands for a steep price, but Vichy patrols watched the jungles and shores, with orders to exterminate any Gaullist camps or deserters attempting to leave the island; a patrol boat discovering one of these illicit ferries would not hesitate to blow it from the water.

But no matter. On news of this possibility, young men of Martinique disappeared overnight. On a clear spring morning in

1943, Joby, Manville and Mosole entered their philosophy class-room at the *lycée* to find half the seats empty. Their professor, Monsieur Joseph-Henri, took equal note of this fact.

"Gentlemen, I see we have some absences. Where is Philibert?"

"He joined the Free French Forces on Dominica," came the reply.

Joseph-Henri continued. "Gentlemen, where is Ciceron?"

He received the same answer.

"Where is des Etages?"

Again, the same reply; and so it went as he traversed the room. At last the professor ceased his questioning and stood before them in prolonged thought. "Gentlemen," he said at last. "Your friends have left for war without being ordered to do so."

His grave stare sought every eye.

"Beware, gentlemen: war is a serious thing. Beware, gentlemen: fire burns, war kills. The girlfriends of dead heroes marry men who are happily alive.

"Beware, gentlemen: that which is happening now in Europe is not our concern. It is something else. Be careful, and don't deceive yourselves as to your goals.

"Gentlemen, believe me, when whites kill each other, it is a blessing for the blacks."

The lecture had an impact on Joby, who had deliberated about leaving for Dominica—as had his brothers, and Manville and Mosole and, indeed, every young man still on the island. It was a tough dilemma, especially at this time when the Fanon household had found cause to celebrate their unity in preparation for Félix's wedding.

Some days later, the family traveled north to a chapel in Morne Rouge, an inland town at the base of Mont Pelée, where Félix was to be married. In the midst of strict rationing throughout the island, the family had managed to obtain a cow, two sheep, a pig, and several hens. Nearly two hundred guests were invited, and eagerly awaited a rare evening of indulgence. By early afternoon the families and guests were in high spirits, and Monsieur and Madame Fanon went about their preparations with anxious laughter and banter in anticipation of the first marriage among their children. At around two o'clock the crowd prepared to make their way toward the chapel where the wedding mass would commence. Frantz approached Joby and took him by the arm.

"I have to speak to you," he said. His expression was dry and serious. He led Joby aside and spoke swiftly.

"Joby, I'm leaving in a few hours—tonight—to join the Free French Forces in Dominica."

A silence followed. Joby contemplated the spire of the chapel before him, and at a distance the solid height of the mountain. All he had felt in the preceding instant—all humor, all complacency, all contentment with the day's affairs—fell from him. He might have thought Frantz's statement a joke, had he not known his brother so well. He felt his mouth opening, felt his voice speaking. He heard himself say that it could not be, that it was unthinkable. How could this day of rejoice and kinship be so abruptly forsaken for pursuit of some fantasy, some dream? It was indecent. Frantz defended his decision and a stormy discussion erupted. Finally at a loss to reason further, Joby recalled the lecture of Monsieur Joseph-Henri. He struggled to recite the speech word for word, for he felt certain that if he could speak exactly as Joseph-Henri had spoken then Frantz would be convinced, and his brother would not leave.

When Joby had finished, he looked to Frantz and found an unsparing blaze.

"Joby," said Frantz. "Each time liberty is put in question, we are concerned—whites, blacks, yellows, Kakos. Your professor is a bastard, and I swear to you today that any time and in any place that liberty is threatened, I will commit to it."

Nothing more could be said. Frantz would not be moved. The hard seed of conviction so often planted by his mother's exhortation for family unity had for seventeen years laid roots deep within him and cultivated a determined sense of duty— duty toward a unity that now extended far beyond the family and spread across the oceans to embrace a kin of unknown millions. Frantz had not sought to be persuaded, and his one concern was to know how Joby would explain the absence to their mother, for he knew the family would at once look to Joby as the co-conspirator in Frantz's plans and actions, the one who would abet him and cover up for anything he did. Of course this was true, and they had soon announced the pretext that they were briefly heading down to Saint Pierre, a town sufficiently rebuilt to make it a credible destination for two young men in search of more bread for the wedding banquet.

Joby accompanied his brother as far as Saint Pierre, timidly rebuilt above charred ruins and halfway to the spot where Frantz would steal at nightfall to find passage off the island. The fare demanded by the ferrymen was not inconsiderable, and in ironic adherence to Madame Fanon's insistence on the communal nature of the family, Frantz had swiped and sold some expensive fabric that Monsieur Fanon was saving for a new outfit, and then raided the cashbox of his mother's boutique to make up the rest of the sum. Frantz confessed as much to his brother as they talked, and also confessed fears about the journey to Dominica—tales abounded of ferry captains who took money from dissidents and then cast them into the sea, either in spite or in haste to return to the shore and find another fare. The two brothers then parted ways, and Frantz left his brother with only a keepsake of words.

"One must constantly, Joby, put one's life in accord with one's ideas. No excuse is allowable, or one becomes nothing but a worthless bastard."

On his return to the chapel in Morne Rouge the first person Joby encountered was Madame Fanon.

"Where is Frantz?" she asked.

Joby told her they were unable to get bread in Saint Pierre, and Frantz had gone on to Prêcheur to find some. At this explanation she let Joby alone, but he soon found himself questioned from all sides by Félix, the bride, and his sisters, all of whom noticed the absence at once. Many had their suspicions that Frantz might soon be leaving, and an unspoken sorrow shadowed the festive atmosphere as the air filled with the words, "Have you seen Frantz? Have you seen Frantz?" In the meanwhile Joby stood quietly by. At six-thirty the ceremony began, and still Frantz had not appeared. Madame Fanon approached Joby again.

"Joby, you have lied to me. Where is Frantz?"

Joby commenced a reply, but then merely swallowed and looked away. In the surrounding commotion the crowd stirred in revelry, its murmur rising to fill the high chapel arches with vacant echoes of cheer. Madame Fanon breathed deep in the space of her son's silence and lay a solemn regard on the rood spread far aloft.

"Today I've lost two children," she said in resign. "Félix who has married, and Frantz who has left—God only knows where."

Church at town center, Fort-de-France.
(Photo by author)

4

Motherland

It is solely by risking life that freedom is obtained.

—Hegel

The journey to Dominica was long and perilous—the small open boat precariously overloaded and the ocean current violently heaving—but the seventeen-year-old's adventurous escape to the island was quite the opposite. On Dominica Frantz received two months of military training, but discovered that the liberation struggle on British Caribbean islands amounted to a great deal of sitting around, awaiting orders from some unspecified higher authority that never seemed to come.

In the spring of 1943, shortly after Frantz arrived on Dominica, the United States at last recognized Martinique as an outpost for Nazi submarine activity, and abruptly discontinued economic trade with the island. The embargo had an immediate impact on Martinique and other French islands under Vichy rule that had previously depended upon United States support for supplies they could no longer get from Europe. This uncomfortable deprivation, in conjunction with mounting public antagonism against Admiral Robert that culminated in civilian demonstrations tactfully orchestrated by a Gaullist infantry colonel, at last drove Admiral Robert to capitulate and leave the island, taking his aircraft carrier, his submarines and cruisers, and his unwanted sailors back to the open sea they had came from four years before.

Equally deprived by the embargo, the Fanon family suffered more the lack of their lively son, and accommodated his absence with the presence of an afflicted humor. (Monsieur Fanon at times remarked, "Oh yes, your son Frantz—he took my outfit to go rescue the French, while here I am doomed to wearing these old rags!") Hence they were all the more grateful for word of the peaceful landing on the island made by liberation forces, in which their son returned among a thousand Free French troops singing and yelling in proclamation of victory. On news of the island's liberation, De Gaulle sent a general from Algiers, Henri Hoppenot, to act as high commissioner and reestablish the French Republic in the Caribbean. On Bastille Day Hoppenot stood on a platform in the center of the *Savane*, surrounded by thousands of Martinicans crowded in the mid-summer heat, to announce the return of the French Republic to Martinique. Cheers abounded, and hats came off to the swelling tune of the *Marseillaise*.

Frantz had returned to the family, but not for long. The two-month training camp on Dominica had hardly satisfied Frantz's desire to prove his commitment to ideals of liberty, and the taste of freedom earned by the defeat of Admiral Robert served to convince the youth of Martinique that tyranny could in fact be defeated, and that hope remained for salvation of the motherland. A great deal of nationalist sentiment overcame the youth of the island—for *their* France, the good France, still suffered from an occupation not unlike what they had endured for four long years, and while France remained subjected, they could not feel truly free. In response, hundreds of Martinique's bourgeois youth volunteered to join the liberation struggle in North Africa with the intent to push

Hitler's forces back into Germany. Frantz, Manville and Mosole were among the first volunteers.

Frantz had only completed the first part of his exams for the baccalaureate at the *lycée*, and managed to complete the oral portion of the exams successfully after his return, unnecessarily aided by the relaxed attitudes of professors during this brief period of public rapture on the island. Joby, now teaching primary school, again attempted to persuade Frantz to change his mind about leaving to fight, but again found all persuasion futile in the face of Frantz's unbending conviction and determination. And few would be swayed when parades of heroic volunteers led by trumpeting bands marched every street in Fort-de-France, to the great cheer and admiration of the crowds. As for Félix, his new wife was with child, and the child would be the first of a new generation. Frantz suggested that she name the child after him; in case he did not return from the war, she could thereby remember him.

Spring of 1944 brought the day of departure. The volunteer army, living in makeshift barracks at the *lycée* above the city, had been informed by High Command they would be given a single, grand parade on the morning they shipped off, in which they would march the streets of the city before their families and friends and then receive an honorable farewell from city officials gathered on the *Savane*. In lieu of this plan, Frantz, Manville and Mosole found themselves roused from the barracks at three in the morning and marched only as far as the harbor to leave under cover of night. Despite the attempt at a secret departure, word soon brought half the town from their beds, and families arrived to cry and wave and bid the young, stoic soldiers goodbye. At the gangplank Madame Fanon held her son in her arms, and in a quivering voice offered instructions on how he might protect himself from "the German fiends." She turned to Manville and said, with all tearful hope she could muster, "You watch out for Frantz, Marcel. You are the oldest. I'm entrusting him to you." Though rarely at a loss for words, Manville found difficulty surpassing the lump in his throat to tell her not to worry, and timidly promised he would take care of her son and return him safely. The young men then turned and boarded the S.S. *Orégon*, a merchant ship converted to transport twelve hundred fledgling soldiers across the Atlantic. From the deck of the ship through the morning mist they watched their families, their town, and their island disappear.

While all of the soldiers felt bitter resentment at being cheated of the promised ceremony, Frantz was livid. It was exactly this type of injustice—an injustice that forced him to subjugate his own wishes to an unchallengeable authority—that he could not bear, and that roused in him the deepest rancor. The ship had hardly left the harbor when Frantz launched into a tirade concerning the handful of white officers who stood haughtily on the deck above the twelve hundred black conscripts, and declared that he would, as an act of protest, demand of the ship's command that they pull down the French flag and fly a black flag in its place. Manville and Mosole watched with stunted amusement as he paused in his rant, and then, after a breath, proclaimed another thing: he would also insist they change the name of the boat from the *Orégon* to the *Banfora*.

The young men laughed, but soon fell silent.

In the channel to Dominica an Allied warship came alongside and escorted the *Orégon* on its daylong voyage to Bermuda. There, not far beyond the coast of the Florida peninsula, they marveled on deck as the two ships made pace with a blazing armada of two thousand vessels that speckled the water as far as could be seen; mammoth warships and submarines and aircraft carriers whose steel bellies sustained over a million soldiers in passage to war, and would carry on their return the coffins of many. Yet in the summer blue they were seized by this spectacular dream. Fear and incertitude that had silenced the day's uneasy journey gave way to surgings of reverence and pride. The splendor of the scene confirmed they had forsaken their homes to ride in the wake of a magnificent and worthy crusade. Men formerly silent in morbid self-reflection now looked to one another with fraternal recognition. Stomachs of the seasick calmed. The unknown ocean lay wide and open before them.

The brilliance of that first day was soon forgotten for the miserable two weeks at sea that followed. The *Orégon* was overcrowded and undernourished. As the lower quarters were overrun with sick and disagreeable passengers, Fanon, Manville and Mosole slept on deck under a leaky canvas canopy that served more for shade than shelter. They resigned themselves to feeling damp, cold, tired and hungry. With cool revulsion they watched officers attempt to take advantage of island women from the small group of female volunteers. Many recruits were outraged, and though these French officers were no longer the brute charges of Admiral Robert, they bore a discomforting similarity to the former tyrants of the Vichy navy. But for all this not one of the three thought twice as to the rightness of the cause they now pursued—to fight the racist principles of the Nazis—and they retained their enthusiasm and the bantering sense of humor that so easily came in one another's company. As they neared the coast of Africa they discussed the slaveship voyages of their ancestors, and agreed they would refuse to disembark at any point south of the Sahara.

The resolution was never tested. One morning they awoke to find they had entered the immense port of Casablanca; the ship had arrived in Morocco. The soldiers had hardly time to feel the stable land beneath their legs before they were loaded into a truck and driven south to a camp at Guercif—a veritable Babel for all the languages and cultures found among the twenty thousand troops stationed there. The various armies of France, Algeria, Tunisia, Senegal and Chad were not only represented, but stratified into a complex and edifying social structure that made the class structure of Martinique seem simple. The camp was divided into numerous zones, and the three Martinicans became intrigued by the methods the military used to segregate one "class" of people from another. For example, among the French whites, soldiers who had come from France were clearly favored to those colonials who came from settlements in Morocco or Algeria, and both groups were favored over the Muslims of North Africa or blacks from the southern regions of Africa.

The clearest demarcation was not one of race, but a distinction made between "Europeans" and "natives"—with the word "native" serving essentially to signify anyone the European command deemed insignificant. Certain African communities in Senegal were considered more "civilized" by the French, and blacks from these areas counted as Europeans, as were citizens of the "old colonies" in the French West Indies, which included the Martinicans. The remaining population were lumped together as natives—a designation that came with a preordained reputation of men who were liars, thieves, alcoholics, and generally dim-witted—and were forbidden from entering the European zone. Though Fanon, Manville and Mosole slept in the European camp and were fed "civilized" European cuisine, their sleeping quarters were not nearly as comfortable as those of the whites.

Fanon took to carrying a notebook around to record these observations, though he seemed less inclined to write in it than to discuss his thoughts with Manville or Mosole, who became sounding boards for his first foray into social theory. The three spent much time in heated discussion, and could hardly miss the irony of the complex racial stratification that had been implemented under the guise of an army that would fight in the name of brotherhood and equality for all humankind. A point of particular indignation for all three concerned the red berets they were forced to wear as European blacks to distinguish themselves from the Africans. A black soldier was not allowed to enter the European camp without a beret on his head, and if he forgot to wear it he could expect "a kick in the ass" and an angry lecture from the adjutant officer for the disrespect this oversight supposedly revealed. Fanon laughed with a mixture of disgust and disbelief at the thought that his only assurance of respect at the camp rested in wearing a hat.

The three Martinicans were given plenty of time to discuss their observations, and to endure the most excruciating boredom on top of everything. Finally, after two months at Guercif, the announcement came of a Gaullist high official arriving at the camp. Three hundred troops were lined up for inspection. When the official asked if there were any complaints or questions, three hands came up: Fanon, Manville and Mosole.

Immediately after the official made private appointments to meet with the three men, they found themselves intercepted by four commanding officers who ushered them into an office.

"Don't say a thing," Manville whispered to the others.

Behind their stony expressions, the three men were now having the best time yet in their army career. Manville struggled to keep a straight face. The four interrogating officers grilled them regarding their intended complaints, but the interrogation proved fruitless. The men would not speak. The officers finally gave up their questioning and resorted to an implied reward if the three recruits would promise to give a positive report. The three men then left the exasperated officers, having followed Manville's advice to the letter.

Once in the office of the visiting official, each of the three aired his grievance about the unfair conditions in the camp and the thoroughly racist treatment the majority of soldiers were made to endure. Worst of all, they endured it quietly and with almost no sense of purpose, having received no sign that they would ever get to contribute to the war effort, which at this point was being fought mostly in Europe and far from their base in southern Morocco. The official nodded considerately at each complaint, and several days later an order arrived to move the entire battalion from southern Morocco to the town of Bougie on the northern coast of Algeria.

The three men were quite satisfied at having chosen to speak up, but their satisfaction soon dissipated as they passed into southern Algeria and witnessed the rampant devastation left by the Nazis in their retreat from North Africa the previous year. The country was left utterly impoverished, stripped of the most basic necessities. Famine and disease were epidemic. All humanity seemed lost, and Fanon had never seen anything like it. He watched with cool contempt as soldiers provoked fights among Algerian children simply by tossing out crusts of bread. The scene affected Manville and Mosole as well, but Fanon seemed to close in on himself at the sight of such wretched conditions. At one point they stumbled upon a group of small children digging through the trash, and Fanon flew into a rage. He charged at the children and yelled for them to get out of the garbage before he killed them. Then he returned to his companions stiff-lipped, and they silently went on.

Standing at the docks in Bougie one could imagine a view of the southern coast of France directly across the Mediterranean; and though the soldiers were now tantalizingly close to the real action of the war, it seemed as far away as ever. The change in location had scarcely changed or mitigated the racism they suffered at the hands of the French army, and the presence of an "officer candidate school" in Bougie—whose candidates were chosen exclusively from white French bourgeoisie who wore their candidate uniforms around town with an imperious air—caused the three Martinicans to shake their heads all the more. They coped with the authoritarian regime in the same rebellious way they had always coped with fatuous authority, and the file records for "Fanon, Frantz," "Manville, Marcel" and "Mosole, Pierre" grew thicker by day with reports of the minor infractions and breaches of authority committed by each.

In the course of their stay in North Africa, Fanon had become more intrigued by the situation he found there, and grew steadily more aware of the deleterious effects of colonialism he had heretofore avoided in the relatively tepid colonial climate of Martinique. In Bougie he made occasional sorties beyond the sheltered military zone to try to make contact with the local population. To his consternation, he was shunned. While he fancied he might establish a certain kinship with the local population in Algeria—who were, like himself, non-European citizens of a French colony—instead he was astonished to find they wanted nothing to do with him. He reached the conclusion that North Africans despised men of color. For just as the black petite bourgeoisie of Martinique had regarded the blacks of Guadeloupe and Saint Lucia as uncultured bumpkins, so did the Muslims of French North Africa harbor a similar prejudice against other Africans. Fanon felt hurt by these rejections, to be sure—he was too sensitive to feel otherwise, and he had yet to comprehend the social and psychological complexities at work in a colonized people. Still, the discomforting incidents stuck in his mind, and set him to working on a problem of human psychology that would later consume his career.

For most of the summer the three men had only one another,

French soldiers march through Algiers.
(Algerian National Press and Information Documentation Center)

and beneath their long, impassioned ideological debates they developed an insular interdependency, often sparked with playful aggravation. Vacant and pointless hours left Frantz with a perennial feeling of agitation, and his only escape was to enlist a companion with whom to share observations and discussions. He hated to go out alone and was timid when it came to making new friends, so Manville and Mosole were often obliged to join him. One evening the latter two could not be motivated to accompany Fanon to the cinema to see the latest film, and after a fair amount of urging, he announced that he would simply go alone. A couple hours later he came tearing back into the room and proclaimed that he had seen the most incredible film: it was all about jazz music, and all of the musicians that Manville and Mosole dearly admired. The film had left him so excited that the other two decided to see it at once, and rushed off to catch the next showing. On their return they found him equally exhilarated, only this time he was doubled over with taunting laughter. A minute passed in which he was the only one laughing, for he had just tricked them into watching the most tediously boring love story that any of them had ever seen.

The early weeks of June in 1944 had brought about the Allied invasion of France, beginning with the D-Day landings at Normandy. A few weeks into the campaign, a meeting of the French troops was called at Bougie and a colonel announced that a second invasion of Europe was planned to push the Nazis up from the south. The fighting could be vicious, and it was already decided that the first landing from the French division would be made by the Senegalese (for everyone knew what the Senegalese were so vehemently told: "You are the best soldiers in the French Empire"). But, the colonel announced, if anyone among the French troops—what the Senegalese would call the *Toubabs*—

wished to fight in the first wave, they were free to volunteer. To their surprise, there were three West Indian *Toubabs* who were eager to go.

Following an air campaign that heavily bombarded the coast, landings for Operation Dragoon along the Côte d'Azur commenced on the fifteenth of August with three American divisions, followed by the French. Fanon, Manville and Mosole were three among ten West Indian volunteers who fought alongside the Sixth Regiment of Senegalese Troopers, commanded by Colonel Raoul Salan. Frantz, now nineteen, was the youngest of the ten. Roused from their cots at three in the morning, they crossed the Mediterranean in a fleet of Allied landing craft carrying six thousand troops to land at the bay of Saint-Tropez on the southern shore of France. Despite the ominous gray of the morning, the shore was quiet and devoid of fighting. Many German troops had been called away to assist in the defense of northern France against the Normandy invasion, and the remainder had orders from Berlin to retreat to a defense line running from Sens to Dijon. Only scattered patrols remained. The Allied troops warily traveled the empty road toward Toulon, and there they met their first rounds of gunfire. By Monday, the twenty-eighth, the city was secured.

They pursued the retreating Germans north along the Rhone River through Avignon and across hilly meadows, with snow-covered Alps aspiring high to the east. One night Fanon was given sentry duty, and he sat awake with watchful disquiet in the darkness while the others slept. In the late hours he was at last relieved of duty, and made his way down the hill to join the resting patrol. At once the jarring cracks of machine-gun fire put every man on his feet, rifle in hand, and they darted up the hill to where the shots were heard. When they reached the top the shooting had ceased, the stalking Germans had disappeared, and

Fanon's replacement, on watch for only minutes, lay dead.

Such early brushes with death begged deeper reflection regarding his own life and the people who had made a difference in it. Frantz sent numerous heartfelt letters back to Martinique, most especially to his mother, Joby and Gabrielle. The extremity of his circumstance led him to say exactly what passed his mind, leaving little unsaid. To his Uncle Edouard he confessed,

> Edouard, you were the vertebral column of my ascension. I read the book you recommended. Polyeucte was right. I am in the wrong. . . .

For his father, his missives were less flattering:

> Papa, you were sometimes very inferior in your duty as a father. If I permit myself to so judge you, it is because I no longer belong to this earth. . .

Indeed, as they passed through lowland towns razed by Nazi destruction, there was plenty for Frantz to reflect upon, and ample time for reflection. Without gasoline, the troops marched twenty to thirty miles a day along the route of Napoleon, passing northeast of Lyon by early September. A few days later they approached the primary German defense line on the road to Besançon, and there hit heavy resistance. An entrenched machine-gun nest held them at bay. A group of Senegalese were ordered to take out the nest. Three attempts met with mortal failure. Fanon heard a Senegalese mutter in wonder as to why they didn't send in any *Toubabs* to attack the nest. He felt a pang of guilt in the presumption that he was a *Toubab*, and thought the comment was directed at him. Later, when the fighting subsided, he realized the absurdity of this assumption—all blacks were "natives" to the French commanders; at this point, no one cared where he was from.

They drove the Germans east of Besançon, and fought a heavy battle at Montbéliard as they approached the region of Alsace. Frantz was grazed by a German bullet that took him from the action for a few days. Most soldiers viewed this type of minor wound as a blessing and a chance to escape the fighting, and many found any excuse to prolong their recovery periods. Fanon, on the contrary, was eager to return to the battlefield. He returned with an infuriated, ruthless energy.

The three Martinicans had become separated at this point, and after the battle tried to get word of one another's well-being. As they pushed further north in October and winter advanced upon the troops, a decision was made to reorganize the division in preparation for the coming cold. Only Europeans, it was believed, could really endure a European winter. An order was sent out to "whiten" the division, and troops from tropical climates were sent back to the south of France for the more temperate weather. But as the Senegalese were ordered to pack up and return to the coast, Fanon, Manville and Mosole found themselves completely overlooked. These men of the 'old colonies' were Europeans; it was only the African natives who could not stand the cold, and the men from the tropic West Indies remained. Their fluent command of French had somehow given them resistance to the lower temperatures.

November brought on a bitter winter, and many men marched on frostbitten feet along the icy Doubs River. Temperatures would reach thirty below zero. The young French soldiers who had replaced the Senegalese straggled behind in the snow, and the West Indians took pride in heading the front of the line. If they were made to overcome the cold, by God, they would overcome it without concession. In response to his many letters home, Frantz received a letter from his mother as they approached Alsace, the region of her birth, still held fast by German forces. It was her custom to sign letters to her children with the phrase, "Your mother, who prays for you," and the children knew that she did in fact pray for them with all earnest. But as Frantz rested his legs in the biting cold and read his mother's letter of news from home and urgings of caution, he read the final page to find that she had signed, "Your mother, who marches with you." His chest swelled as he felt her presence there, in the whole of her great spirit, marching within him. From that moment they pressed on, and Frantz resolved to take extra care of himself, as he now carried an invaluable cargo.

Through the deep wintry woods they pressed north to Belfort. There the Nazis struck back from the mountain crests of the Vosges, and a fierce counterattack escalated into what would become the Battle of Alsace. The Allies were forced into defensive positions, and were soon running desperately low on provisions and artillery. A small party was needed to traverse the difficult and snowy terrain open to German fire and deliver ammunition to the forward line. Fanon volunteered to lead the mission. Their valiant efforts came off a success, but Fanon was badly wounded by a mortar shell, taking shrapnel in his chest and shoulder.

He was treated at a hospital at Nantua, a small town near Geneva on the French-Swiss border, some miles northeast of Lyon. His injuries had been fairly grave, and this time there would be no immediate return to the field. His convalescence lasted nearly two months—though this is hardly to propose that the hospital could keep him at rest for so long. Not a couple weeks passed before Fanon was sneaking out to a nearby soccer field to play with a local team against teams from Lyon. Perhaps to prevent his mother from worrying, he did not write about his injury to anyone except Uncle Edouard, and assured him it was nothing to worry about.

As soon as he was permitted to travel, he left Nantua to finish his convalescence in Paris—his first opportunity to explore the city so mythically spoken about in his younger days. But though residents of Paris now reveled in their regained liberation, honoring those who had fought for their freedom, Frantz began to make note that he was so rarely included among the honored, and that the ignorant attitudes he had endured at the hands of the French military were equally prevalent among civilians. At social functions women assembled around Americans and British, while Frantz watched idly from the bar. Here he had marched, here he had fought, here he had lain with searing shards beneath his flesh—and yet it seemed only the shade of that flesh gained him any attention, and a most unwanted attention at that.

Though Paris had its charms, the inner isolation and lack of activity brought on pangs of yearning for his family. From Paris he at last wrote his mother:

> Dear little mother, I know you are going to write me, and you will tell me about all that is dear to me, that is, of that table where the reunited family will commune again without a thought. . . . You can imagine the joy one feels on coming home, finding it warm and full of familiar faces. . . .

The one event that took some sting from the bite of his mounting despair came in early February when he was awarded the *Croix de guerre*, with a bronze star and silver palms, bestowed by Colonel Raoul Salan, Commander of the Sixth Regiment of Colonial Infantry, for "brilliant conduct during operations in the valley of the Doubs." He was promoted to corporal, and a few days later he rejoined his unit in Alsace, where the Germans had at last been run out of the *Poche de Colmar*, a pocket of heavily defended German forces near the Rhine at Colmar. Now camped along the shores of the Rhine, the moving river brought daily thoughts of his mother. But still he had not received a letter for some time. He wrote her once more, promising to return to her and not to leave again, and asked her to scold Gabrielle, Joby and Marie-Flore for not writing him more often. Félix, he complained, had not written once. But a few days later he received a letter from Joby that touched and overwhelmed him. He responded with good humor, offering a slightly satirical description of his medal, and alluded to the horrors he had witnessed and the disgust he now harbored toward the entire predicament. His descriptions of the scene were minimal on the premise that men who survived war did not discuss it. "Listen," he wrote Joby, "I have become older than you." Of their two companions, he offered the consoling remark, "Reassure yourself that Pierre Mosole and Manville were still alive a week ago."

At the open of March in 1945, General Eisenhower had a single goal for Allied forces in France and Belgium: to push the Nazis back behind the Rhine from their northernmost positions in Belgium to their southernmost positions just north of Fanon's division in Alsace. The primary thrust was led by General Montgomery in the north, and by the first Wednesday evening in March the Allies had seized the city of Cologne on the west bank of the river. For the French forces in the south, the advance was not as smooth. Moving north along the Rhine, Fanon's division had pursued the Germans northeast as far as Zweibrücken, but just beyond this small town the enemy turned and held firm. The third week in March was a difficult fight for French forces as they struggled to push a well-entrenched German line to either the north or the east, hoping to force this last division in Alsace back across the Rhine. Then on the first day of spring the

Germans received an unwelcome surprise: From the north appeared a triumphant General Patton with five divisions of American soldiers, who had reached the Rhine at Coblenz and then turned south to attack the last Nazi division from the rear. Within a few days there was no more German resistance, and west of the Rhine was entirely in Allied hands.

France was liberated.

A final phase remained for the war against Germany on the western front: to cross the Rhine, and then move deep into Germany towards Berlin. The crossing of the Rhine would entail the biggest military operation since the D-Day invasion at Normandy, and great quantities of assault crafts and bridge materials had been collected in preparation. Incessant air bombardment on Western Germany preceding the invasion ensured that the regions just east of the Rhine would mark the Germans' last battleground against Allied attack from the west. A successful crossing of the river meant a successful road to Berlin. On the twenty-fourth of March the attack commenced in the North, and the invasion continued successfully along the banks southward as one Allied division after another crossed the Rhine into Germany.

The last army to cross was the First French Army in the far south at Speyer and Germersheim, led by General de Lattre de Tassigny, on the thirtieth of March. It was also on this day, just when the Rhine had been crossed by French forces, that the French command "realized" its error in having failed to send the West Indians south for the winter along with the African troops. On this day the division was whitened again. Fanon, Manville and Mosole, and any other West Indians—who constituted the remaining blacks in the French division—were sent back across the Rhine to return to the Côte d'Azur, while the remaining French forces made road to Berlin, and to victory.

Residents of Algiers cheer the arrival of Allied forces.
(AP/Worldwide Photos)

The hill behind Frantz Fanon's house
in downtown Fort–de–France.
(Photo by author)

5

Return Home

> . . . I am the project
> of the recovery of my being.
>
> —*Jean-Paul Sartre*

OWING TO THEIR COURAGEOUS ACTIONS in battle, Marcel Manville and Pierre Mosole had also been awarded the *Croix de guerre*, and all three men had achieved the rank of corporal by the time they returned to the beaches at Toulon, where they had landed the preceding August. In seven months they had learned and experienced a great deal: Both Manville and Mosole told of their own experiences of alienation that were similar to what Fanon had endured in Paris. And already they had some inkling of how ungrateful their great colonial motherland could be, bronze star or no. Their remaining stay in Toulon would only drive home this painful fact all the more.

Their arrival was initially pleasant, as they reunited with other West Indians from the battalion who had not been heard from in months. In early April, with the war closing on multiple fronts, the port city now filled with soldiers of every nationality and from every arena of the European struggle. The impending end to the fighting fostered a general air of relief and merriment, and celebrations abounded. American soldiers returning from the war against Mussolini brought back Italian prisoners of war who were detained at the American base, and who, the West Indians at once noticed, were offered better living conditions than the French army offered its own black "heroes."

And these heroes were snubbed in many ways to come. The general population, they soon noticed, would hardly speak to them except in the most condescending tones. At the victory balls young French women swarmed around the Americans— who offered them chocolate and chewing gum—and ignored the three decorated corporals who had only their stories and battle scars to offer. Requests to dance were answered with appalled rejections, if not with reflexive fear and gestures of flight. Yet they watched as those same women gladly danced with Italian prisoners of war. Fanon, Manville and Mosole were soon thoroughly disgusted. To be mistreated at the hands of the ignorant military was one thing, but until now they had never felt so offended. These men who had fought for the equality of races would realize with all bitterness that they had achieved nothing of the sort, and in their solitary contempt wished only to return to the West Indies and describe how the great motherland had called them to fight in its name, and then turned its back on them when the fighting was finished.

On the twelfth day of April, a day when Allied forces crossing Germany liberated the Buchenwald and Belsen concentration camps, a day when President Franklin Roosevelt succumbed to a long struggle against ailing health and President Truman was sworn into office to succeed him, a day when the world held its breath in anticipation of the coming fall of Berlin and the imminent death of Hitler, Frantz Fanon wrote his parents in bitter reconsideration of his youthful ideals:

Today, April 12. One year since I left Fort-de-France. Why? To defend an obsolete ideal. . . . If I don't return, if you learn one day of my death facing the enemy, console yourselves, but don't ever say: he died for a good cause. Say: God called him back; for this false ideology of lay schoolteachers, of ignorant laymen and politicians, must no longer illuminate us. *I was mistaken. . . .*

Most West Indians in Toulon felt equally bitter, and Fanon and the others made no effort to hide their mounting displeasure. It was not long before word traveled the chain of command about these angry faces dampening the festivities, and a decision was made that the best thing to do was to send all of the West Indians back to where they had come from.

Because the war had destroyed most seaports along the southern coasts of France, the soldiers endured a long and exhausting journey to Rouen, along the Normandy coast, where they were put up in a defunct chateau at Bois-Guillaume. The chateau overlooked a splendid park, and as autumn approached the young men availed themselves of its sprawling grasses by playing soccer and again revisiting the joys of youthful abandon.

The town itself was strange to them, a coastal suburbia populated with green lawns and reserved, quiet people. By this point they had learned better than to attempt any interaction with the local townspeople, instead contenting themselves with one another's company and with the pleasures of the great chateau that was temporarily at their disposal. But one morning brought a pleasant surprise when the captain of the company called them together to announce that a local merchant, an important businessman of the area, had heard about their presence in the chateau and expressed his desire to meet the young West Indian troops who had traveled such a great distance to fight in the struggle for French liberation. Furthermore, to facilitate an intimate gathering, he had decided to invite them in groups of fifteen for dinner in their honor at his house. The soldiers were stupefied. Never in their travels through France, through all the towns they had marched, never had townspeople thought to speak to them, let alone offer an expression of thanks and an invitation to dinner. It was a stunning but welcome event.

Much needed to be decided before the first dinner. To begin with, who would be the first fifteen to go? The captain revealed that he himself had already decided this matter, and produced a list of fifteen names he believed to best represent the troop: all of them were well-spoken graduates of secondary school, educated sons of lawyers and civil servants; in short, an elite selection that was certain to offer the most distinguished impression from those among their lot in the eyes of a prominent French businessman. At the top of his list were the three most intelligent and well-spoken men among them: Fanon, Manville and Mosole. Even after this discriminating process of selection, the captain took the fifteen men aside and offered a solemn lecture on how they should conduct themselves, keeping in mind that the businessman had a wife and three daughters who would be eating at the table as well. But the men did not need to be told such things; of course they would conduct themselves in exactly the manner their families had taught them to. Still, the captain appeared somewhat nervous, and not until the evening of the dinner did they hear him remark that this would be the first time that a prominent Normandy family would eat at the same table with "men of color." For Fanon and Manville, the remark caught them off guard. Could nothing transpire on French soil without attention to race being at issue?

The army drove them to the house and dropped them at the door of the family cottage. Cottage! In fact, the house was a veritable chateau, and all the more enchanting inside, where they were led to an immense dining room decorated with flowers around a long table with twenty elegant place settings. They had entered a fairy tale. The host was in his fifties, a polite businessman who was not remarkably political, but who had nevertheless fought in the resistance during Vichy occupation. His wife was charming, his three teenage daughters beautiful and sociable, and hardly had they seated themselves before the soldiers felt dignified and appreciated—as they should have felt long ago. Any lingering bitterness toward the French now receded. The women in Toulon who refused to dance with them, forgotten. For here, at last, was their France: Here was the France they had learned of in school, and the French they had imagined worth fighting for. The *real* French!

Marcel found himself particularly enchanted by a redheaded daughter, and could hardly decline when the others asked him to display his verbal adroitness in a speech expressing their gratitude; for he was given to launching into long, eloquent discourse, and took a great deal of pride in this fact. When he tactfully dared an inquiry as to why they had been invited, their host plainly replied that though he had fought in the resistance, he believed greater thanks were due to the soldiers who had left their homes and traveled so far to risk their lives in defense of a cause that did not really concern them, while the sons of many French families remained at home in fainthearted apathy. The soldiers accepted this response with a humble quiet, but sitting at the table Fanon and Manville now harbored a prideful sense of justification at the choice they had made two years earlier—a choice they had often doubted before this moment. Now their pride at last returned. With equal tact, the host made his own inquiry: Why, among the fifteen soldiers, did he find only men with diplomas destined for positions as doctors, lawyers and civil servants? Did the West Indies not produce soldiers who were fishermen, or construction workers, or farmers? Little could be said save the truth, and the soldiers kindly admitted they had stacked the deck in their own favor, hoping to make a good impression. With an accepting chuckle, the host announced that for the next group he would have to ask the captain for fifteen men without diplomas, who would not be doctors or lawyers, but who had fought alongside them with equal devotion. His point was well taken. Still, the next day the fifteen veteran diners requested of their captain that *they* be allowed to choose the next fifteen to go, and proceeded to spend the day giving the next group a supplemental lesson on how they ought to behave, so the family would see that West Indians knew how to conduct themselves, no matter what their origin or walk of life.

As for Frantz, reminiscence of his discussion with Joby before his departure, and of his bitter letter home, left him to wonder if perhaps he had not been mistaken after all.

In early October seven hundred soldiers from Martinique, Guadeloupe and Guyana left Rouen to board the S.S. *San-Matéo* for the return trip home. As they boarded the ship they were bid a cheering adieu by a crowd of men, women and children from the area who appeared at the docks to display gratitude and affection for their West Indian liberators. It was an encouraging send-off, and the soldiers made their way aboard with dreams of similar cheering crowds that would welcome the heroes on their arrival home. They would place their medals on their bureaus and deservedly gloat, avenged of the shameful departure the local authorities had inflicted upon them eighteen months before. As always, their satisfaction was short-lived. The ship the army had chosen to transport their soldiers home was far from glamorous or even respectable: In fact, it was a rusty tub of old motors used for transporting livestock, and it had scarcely been retrofitted to carry people. They were, in essence, livestock of a different kind: the military kind. Crammed into dirty and nauseating cubicles and fed corned beef and old biscuits, these proud survivors of a brutal war wondered if they would survive the trip home; and if so, if they would have to be carried from the boat on stretchers. They generally agreed that the army had chosen to punish them, though for what they could not imagine. It was a three-week sentence in the most dismal prison they could imagine.

When at last they arrived home, the familiar bay beneath its tropic skyline coming to view at a slow clip, the *Savane* with its tamarind palms waving leisurely, no fanfare awaited them. The island officials had made no note of their arrival, and only their families showed up at the docks to greet them. On their discharge from the army, the only gifts they received were the backpacks they had shouldered in the bitter cold from one end of France to the other. Welcome-home parties were limited to family gatherings arranged by their parents, reunions with uncles, cousins, and old friends. Still, they were home at last— the place they had wished to be for so long. The men spent time with family and friends, took rowboats out on the ocean and swam in the cool water, and took walks through warm, open fields. They were home and alive, and life was good.

But life also pressed on. Not many days of relaxation passed before the young veterans were compelled to consider the future. Around him Frantz noticed that things were nearly the same as when he had left: Joby was still teaching primary school, and Félix worked to support his new family, now including the new Frantz of the Fanon clan, just learning to walk. Looking at the community he had returned to, Frantz had a difficult time imagining a similar future for himself, as he had seen too much of the world to settle back into that small province he knew from childhood. He seemed at times unsettled and restless, and in many ways a different man. His old playful and troublemaking demeanor was supplanted by a newfound sobriety and coolness. He seemed much older, somewhat despairing, and would scarcely speak of what had passed during the war. He considered the war inappropriate to talk about, though it seemed to haunt him in numerous ways.

At Christmas Manville left Martinique for Paris, with the financial help of his working sisters, to study law at the university. Despite Frantz's written promises never to abandon his family again, he now sympathized with Manville's decision to leave only two months after they had returned. With thoughts of doing something similar, Frantz enrolled in the spring term at the *lycée* to supplement his education, and studied with a renewed seriousness and vigor. He was now quiet and aloof from the other students, and studied with intense focus. The books he read included mostly philosophy and psychology, and he developed a particular predilection for some of the existential philosophers, including Nietzsche, Jaspers, and Sartre. He was particularly inspired by Sartre's book *Anti-Semite and Jew*, published in that year, which presented a brief but compelling psychological analysis of racism. Sartre's words were like a light turned on inside him, and perfectly described his own experiences and observations as a minority in Europe. Inspired by Sartre and Césaire, he once again played with the idea of becoming a dramatist. But he found philosophy and science to be equally engrossing. In truth, he was not sure what he would do.

For the time being, the only real excitement to be found on the island was in a political chasm that was opened by the war. There was much debate over the role this small colonial island would play in the new, post-war French Republic. Many conservatives wanted a return to the status quo of pre-war days, but the younger generation saw an opportunity for change given the turbulent and fragile political environment that existed in France. In the years during the war the Communist party had risen to prominence in Martinique as a result of its importance to the French resistance. And their primary candidate for the

French parliament was none other than Aimé Césaire.

As always, Césaire was outspoken about his ideas for social change on the island, and outspoken in the most compelling manner. His arguments called for a change in Martinique's political status and orientation from that of a passive colony in service of the mainland to that of an active political entity in its own right, concerned above all with the interests of its own people. Thrilled by the idealism and the prospects of change advocated in Césaire's political speeches, and thrilled by the thought that the teacher they so admired was rapidly becoming such an important figure, Frantz and Joby decided to join his campaign. That summer they traveled with Césaire around the entire island, hoping to garner rural support for the need of better infrastructure and self-governance throughout the community. Joby was the first to point out, however, that they never seemed to reach the real countryside, but were always directing their campaign toward residents of the towns and large villages who had fewer agrarian concerns. They discovered that the countryside population was difficult to reach, not only because of their remote locations but because of the scant trust they were willing to place in these city folk who spoke like the *békés* and came promising changes to a seemingly-unchangeable system. Despite these difficulties, Frantz and Joby learned much in the course of the campaign, and heard from Césaire some of the best oration they would ever hear. In Fort-de-France, they watched a woman faint as she became overwhelmed by Césaire's words. In another town, Césaire thundered a speech that neither man would forget:

> When I turn on my radio, when I hear that Negroes have been lynched in America, I say that we have been lied to: Hitler is not dead; when I turn on my radio, when I learn that Jews have been insulted, mistreated, persecuted, I say

that we have been lied to: Hitler is not dead; when, finally, I turn on my radio and hear that in Africa forced labor has been inaugurated and legalized, I say that we have certainly been lied to: Hitler is not dead.

With Césaire yielding such powerful rhetoric as his foremost weapon, it was not difficult to predict who would win the campaign.

At the end of the summer Frantz was at last in a position to leave again to study in Paris. Though his military service won him a scholarship to study whatever he wished, he was still unsure exactly what this might be. Drama was too impractical. He liked the idea of studying medicine, though the time it required seemed to him much too long, and he wasn't sure if his financial situation would allow so many years of schooling. He would still need money simply to live, and he was also faced with the consideration that Joby and Gabrielle wanted to study in France at the same time, and the family's finances could not stretch very far. Joby could save some money from his teaching, but Gabrielle was in a more vulnerable financial predicament.

Another companion destined for Paris was Pierre Mosole, who had decided to study dentistry, which could be a lucrative career that did not require many years for a degree. Frantz considered this possibility, and put in an application to the same dental school. Shortly before he and Gabrielle were to leave (Joby would start the next term), Frantz discussed his financial situation with his mother and, noting that she gave money to Gabrielle for some extra things like handkerchiefs, asked if she might do him the same favor. Madame Fanon flatly said no, with the reasoning that Frantz was better situated than his sister and could handle himself. This was essentially true, but Frantz felt offended. He did not see why his sister needed to go study in

France anyway, and now she was receiving all the favors. But Frantz had never been a remarkable student, Madame Fanon noted, and perhaps he ought to think twice before questioning someone else's choice to continue in school. Against his protests she remained adamant, and as late summer brought their impending departure the disagreement between mother and son dissipated from the air—though it had still to dissipate from memory.

The brevity of Fanon's career as a dental student betrays the seriousness with which he ever considered the idea. After they arrived in Paris and joined Manville, Frantz hardly unpacked his bags before showing up at Manville's door to announce that he was leaving. When asked for an explanation, Frantz replied, "There are too many blacks in Paris." Perhaps the city brought untenable memories of his alienating experience there only a few years before, or more likely he felt too much like another face in a crowd he desired only to get away from. Further prodding by Manville at last unleashed a tirade: The dentistry school was full of idiots—more idiots than he'd ever seen. And it was unbearably boring! Besides, it seemed so trivial to him. Was this to be his life's calling—dentistry? He had always felt destined for something greater. His summer working with Césaire had inspired him all the more; a greater contribution could be made to the world. These old moral voices sounded emphatically again. It was his duty to do something better. So he reached a decision: he would go to medical school after all, and he would become a surgeon. He had decided to enroll for pre-med classes at the university in Lyon—a much cheaper place to live than Paris, and a place where he knew he could find some excellent games of soccer.

After they spent some time discussing their respective futures, Manville escorted his friend down to the Gare Saint Lazare, watched him board the next train to Lyon, and then made an attempt to return to his studies, yet feeling a little distracted.

Pen and ink sketch of Franz Fanon.
(By author)

6

Masks

Every profound spirit needs a mask: even more, around every profound spirit a mask is growing continually, owing to the constantly false, namely shallow, interpretation of every word, every step, every sign of life he gives.

—*Friedrich Nietzsche*

TO LIVE AMONG OTHERS is a quiet tragedy. To live in solitude unmutes the chorus wail. The actors departed from stage, only a song of consciousness remains. Expressions formed for discernment by others—roles played for the drama of scene and relation—dangle in air but lose all immediacy, marking rhythms numinous with an uncanny reason. One's language becomes foreign, one's face the face of a stranger. Questions break through to the surface. To observe Frantz Fanon at age twenty-one, a young man seated on a train from Paris to Lyon, head turned to the window in thought, a curious traveler might inquire many things. Where had he come from? Where would he go? And why choose the one place above the other? All benign questions, to be sure, and common among travelers; but did he not, if one may dare ask, as strangers passing time: did he not seek some escape in this journey? Was he not in fact, to venture a guess in the evening calm, running for his life? On burning heels, even?

Yes, there were too many blacks in Paris. But perhaps it was not the presence of them that disturbed, so much as the existence

Masks: A sculpture in tribute to Frantz Fanon
at the entrance to the University of the Antilles in Schoelcher,
Martinique.
(Photo by author)

of the category; and a category to which one inevitably belonged, whether one desired to or not. A category that identified from a distance, without inquiry, without exchange of a single word.

"Ah! Another black man in Paris! Splendid. Left your little island to get an education, eh? Well you and your friends will have a wonderful time here. I suppose you like jazz music, do you? We have some wonderful little clubs here you know . . . Yes, yes. A fantastic place for a Negro like you, Paris . . . Listen, here's a restaurant I just know you people like . . ."

In Lyon he would escape the typicality of all that, the history of this category that preceded him—a history already owned by Césaire, for one, and Senghor and so many others—and perhaps a fresh trail could be blazed. In Lyon a black man was more a rarity; the medical school at the university enrolled only a few blacks among four hundred students. Offering no pre-ordained niche for him, the city brought a promise of oblivion, an escape from all trace of that burden, the achievement of a blessed ignorance that would allow him to be a man—and no more, and no less. Or so one might wish, though reality offered a different bargain. Perhaps to remain in Paris would have been the more commodious choice; to allow oneself to uncomfortably ease into that category and bear with its distortions in exchange for a false air of belonging. But perhaps, for Fanon, it was exactly this false acceptance that would be the most unbearable, and in his choice of Lyon he assured himself no such peace of mind. Whatever else might await him, his demons were surely there, waiting to face him.

The city of Lyon had its own demons to face. Plagued by strikes in the economic turmoil that followed the war, protests and political strife filled the air day and night. To accommodate the influx of students given a free bill for their military service, the

Minister of Education seized some of the city's larger prostitution houses and converted them to dormitories for the university. Beyond the seizure of property, conversion efforts were minimal, and Fanon and many other students lived in small boudoirs with a bed, a sink, and a bidet. The downstairs lounge, complete with eight-foot mirrors and leather divans, was a welcoming place to study.

Fanon, however, had a difficult time feeling welcome, no matter where he went. Even when he was welcomed with open arms, it was for all the wrong reasons. It became painfully clear that no matter where he fled to, the category could not be escaped. In every encounter he found himself "tucked away" by others, reduced to some pocketable description. His race was invariably remarked upon, whether openly or implicitly. Introductions presented him as "A Martinican, a native of our old colonies." And the next friendly face would offer, "I want you to understand, sir, I am one of the best friends the Negro has in Lyon." It was maddening. It was infuriating. Here he wished only to belong, only to disappear among the crowd, only to lose himself in Frenchness, in whiteness—in all of those aspects he had been taught were superior and beautiful, and yet he was constantly made aware of his difference, constantly reminded, in one way or another, of all the ways he did not possess those aspects, did not belong to that group, and could never belong, no matter what he did. Even his superior command of the French language earned him only the response, "How long have you been in France? You speak French so well."

Undoubtedly, much of this could have been avoided had he remained in Paris. Racism existed in Paris, certainly, but there was also a niche of black students there that would have provided a buffer from it, a tiny haven. But Fanon wanted no haven. He could not bear any haven. As was the case in his childhood and his military service, he needed to seek conflict. The pillar of self-esteem he had built for himself, built with the mortar of will and action, demanded it from him, lest he be nothing but a "worthless bastard." Whether he was working for an authority or against it, he could not feel comfortable without a symbol of authority in his sights. In Lyon he would find only one such authority, an authority that had burned him since the day of his birth: whiteness. And it was an authority that appeared to constantly exclude him from its ranks. For a man as deeply sensitive as Fanon, this fact was unbearably painful.

> I move slowly in the world, accustomed now to seek no longer for upheaval. I progress by crawling. And already I am being dissected under white eyes, the only real eyes. I am *fixed*. Having adjusted their microtones, they objectively cut away slices of my reality. I am laid bare. I feel, I see in those white faces that it is not a new man who has come in, but a new kind of man, a new genus. Why, it's a Negro!

His feelings in this period, the feelings that would soon be put to paper and published as his first book, call out in exasperated anguish, "How do I make them recognize me for what I am, for what I have to give?" Or, as he later wrote with compelling concision, "I shouted a greeting to the world and the world slashed away my joy."

In the midst of these interior conflicts, tragedy struck. In January a telegram from home arrived. Frantz's father was dead. The news was shocking and brutal. He at once took the train to Rouen to be with Gabrielle. With such news coming when he was so far from home, he wanted only to be with family, and of all his sisters he had always felt closest to Gabrielle. Aside from comforting each other, the two siblings had other considerations: The death of their father threw into question the problem of survival for the family. Félix now had his own family to provide for, and Joby, still teaching in Fort-de-France, earned a limited income. The remaining children were still at the *lycée*. Gabrielle proposed to give up her pharmacy studies and find work, but Frantz immediately rejected the idea and, now echoing his mother six months before, lectured her on the importance of her studies until she promised not to quit. Returning to Lyon on the train, he wrote a long letter to his mother in which he described his effort to convince Gabrielle to stay in school. His father's death still seemed strangely unreal to him:

> It is very difficult for one to imagine the death of one's father. . . . Be kind enough, Maman, to send all the details of his death, did he have thoughts of me, you know, one always wants to know what the one who gave you life thinks of you. It's this estimation that henceforth directs your life . . . your daily efforts. . . .

The letter attests to how powerful his father's influence was on Frantz's feelings of worthiness, even in death, when he finds himself evaluating his "daily efforts" according to his father's estimation. Deeply concerned about his mother's future, he pled with her to maintain courage; for herself, and for all her children. He closed the letter by asking her, "Without you, what are we, what are we?"

In the midst of the shock and sadness of his father's sudden death, he continued to seek much inspiration from Madame Fanon, and he wrote home of his successes with a prideful search for approval. His studious efforts in the year of pre-med classes were rewarded by an exemption from exams made for war veterans, so he would be able to move straight to medical school when classes were finished. In a letter home the following November he provided his mother a list of his recent and coming achievements, including his admission to medical school, and promised "a year where only effort should excel." He assured her that the time had passed when teachers complained about him to his father, and when "Mme. Philoctète told you the forfeits of your scoundrel son," wishing his old teachers could see him now. With his father gone, he had adopted the role of the good son. His solemn pledge was, "I will do my best to bring you that deep joy you must feel at our scholarly successes," and vowed to make up all the time he felt he had lost.

In addition to his studies, he found time to take up a great number of extracurricular activities in this period, including the composition of three plays, reminiscent of Césaire, entitled *Les mains parallèles, L'œil se noie*, and *La conspiration (Parallel Hands, The Drowning Eye*, and *The Conspiracy)*. He became involved with several leftist political groups, and enjoyed engaging other students in informal debates in the restaurants and cafés around Lyon. The charge of political turmoil was in the air of the city at the time, with the post-war industrial economy giving rise to daily demonstrations. Though he still struggled with the turmoil of being a black man in a condescending white society, he was given much opportunity to sublimate this struggle into political activity; so much so that it almost endangered his academic career. The year 1947 was an exciting time not only in Lyon, but in much of Fanon's world. Under Césaire's influence, Martinique had just been granted status as a French *département*, and the journal *Présence Africaine* was founded by Alioune Diop. The journal devoted itself to the *négritude* movement, and regularly published Césaire and Senghor, as well as Sartre, Camus, and Gide. Fanon became an avid reader of *Présence Africaine*, finding within its pages a reaffirmation of the identity he now struggled to come to terms with. In the following year Sartre also published his *Orphée Noir* essay that introduced a volume of *négritude* poetry edited by Senghor—an essay which, for Fanon, was fascinating and disturbing. Still, by necessity of the population, most of his friends and associates were white, and likely offered little forum for him to discuss some of the matters most important to him. Even at the latest hours of night his friends knew he could be found somewhere around the converted dormitory surrounded by similar intellectuals, engaged in long verbal critiques of existential philosophy, socialist politics, or even sex. In this way, he seemed truly to enjoy university life.

As had been his fortune at the *lycée*, Fanon also was quick to win the admiration of many women. Sometimes the admirations went unappreciated. One woman was unfortunate enough to remark, "Look how handsome that Negro is!" within earshot of Fanon, to which he promptly and unexpectedly retorted, "Kiss the handsome Negro's ass, Madame!" It was a moment of triumph for him, having finally lashed back at an unwitting collective aggressor that never gave consideration to implications behind its remarks, and the woman was understandably humiliated. Despite such occasional flares of temper, he again found himself with a number of successive girlfriends. Among his fellow students were two intelligent and active women, Josie and Michelle, with whom Fanon could discuss any number of things, and he wound up in a brief affair with the latter. The affair was not lengthy or even very serious, but Fanon would soon discover that Michelle had become pregnant. In light of his overwhelming sense of duty, it is no surprise that Fanon felt obliged to get married. But he was not at all prepared to make such a step, financially or emotionally, and the relationship had never matured that far.

In a confused and agitated state, Fanon took the next train to Paris to discuss the matter with Joby, who had just arrived to commence his studies, and with Manville. Both men told him exactly what he wished to hear: that there was no point in getting married when he did not want to, and that such a step would surely end in disaster. Manville offered counsel that he was not legally obligated to get married, as long as the child was provided for, and Joby emphasized Frantz's continuing responsibility to the child, not only financially but as a supportive father. Returning to Lyon with a renewed perspective on the situation, Fanon supported Michelle through her pregnancy, and was soon the father of a healthy baby girl, whom they named Mireille. Fanon at first wanted the daughter to go live in Martinique, where he felt the child would receive better care from his mother than she would remaining in Lyon, but eventually the plan fell through.

One of the first things Fanon would learn in medical school was that surgery was not his calling. Though quite nimble and dexterous with his feet on a soccer field, the dexterity of his hands was another matter, and he could hardly form precise lines with a pen let alone a scalpel. Moreover, the very procedure of cutting into a cadaver made his hand tremble, enough so that both his professors and fellow students saw fit to keep their distance. But many professors respected him a great deal, at once recognizing him as a superb writer and an incisive thinker. Some even grew to regard him as a colleague, inviting him to their homes for dinner. Others retained a condescending attitude toward him. During exams period, when it was customary for each student to pull a random question from a box, Fanon's turn provoked the professor to ask, "What would you like me to ask you today, son?" Staring at the professor without a word, Fanon plunged his hand into the box.

Not surprisingly, his interests turned to psychiatry. In his spare time he devoured the psychological and existential philosophies of Hegel, Sartre, Jaspers and Lacan. And Nietzsche still topped his list of favorites. Nietzsche's descriptions of the transcendent potential of the human will fit perfectly with Fanon's ideas about the vital importance of his own will. Nietzsche spoke with a particular respect for strength and will in the human spirit that Fanon found readily accessible, endowing the will with power to overcome all obstacles, if only it could achieve the courage and strength to assume that responsibility. For a man like Fanon, who suffered from feelings of weakness and helplessness in the face of a system of society he could not change, an outward commitment to and display of strength and purpose was his only viable means to rise above defeat and regain confidence in his own spiritual nature. From Nietzsche he would obtain a model of not only what a free spirit could be, but also what a free spirit *should* be, and a measure by which to evaluate his own life and the rightness of his own choices. This model was something that he desperately needed, when his former self-evaluations based on a standard of whiteness were being so violently scorched by his experience of the world around him. The images and ideas so crucial to his self-esteem could only be supplanted by symbols of iron dedication and determination, of a spirit that would erupt into transcendence of his everyday experience of himself, of a will so fired to action that it incinerated all uncertainty. During this period he wrote,

When the Negro makes contact with the white world, a certain sensitizing action takes place. If his psychic structure is weak, one observes a collapse of the ego. The black man stops behaving as an *actional* person. The goal of his behav-

Detail of masks at the Forum Frantz Fanon
on the Savane in Fort-de-France.
(Photo by author)

The Forum on the Savane in Fort-de-France,
erected as a tribute by Aimé Césaire, mayor of Fort-de-France.
(Photo by author)

ior will be the Other (in the guise of the white man), for the Other alone can give him worth.

His focus on the role of the Other in the process of self-construction also reveals the affinities he felt with Hegel and Sartre, and this period shows much attention to Sartre's *Being and Nothingness*, another Bible on Fanon's shelf. Sartre's methods of introspection, self-recognition and self-reconstruction could only resemble beautiful music to an intellect like Fanon's:

> Sealed into that crushing objecthood, I turned beseechingly to others. Their attention was a liberation . . . endowing me once more with an agility that I had thought lost . . . But just as I reached the other side, I stumbled, and the movements, the attitudes, the glances of the other fixed me there . . . I was indignant; I demanded an explanation. Nothing happened. I burst apart. Now the fragments have been put together by another self.

As part of this self-reconstruction, and to bolster a sense of his own actional nature, Fanon took on countless responsibilities. In addition to his rigorous studies in medical school, he continued a fair amount of his political dealings, organized a union of students from overseas, and even started his own mimeographed journal, which he entitled *Tam-Tam*. The title arose from the symbol of the tom-tom that permeated several of Césaire's poems and plays, and was often referred to in the pages of his favorite publication, *Présence Africaine*. Dedicated to the literature and theory of *négritude*, most of *Tam-Tam* was written by Fanon himself, and the dissemination of his writing earned him invitations to speak around town. At one lecture he drew a parallel between Black and European poetry, and among the many compliments he received after the lecture, a thrilled acquaintance informed him, "At bottom you are a white man."

His attempts to escape this kind of categorization—as he had attempted when leaving Paris for Lyon—had long been abandoned as futile. There would be no escape save within, and writing became his greatest salvation. A large portion of his first book was written in spurts of energy in 1949 and 1950, a time that was increasingly difficult for Fanon. Despite the clarity of mind the book exhibits, he was understandably wrought with confusion and self-doubt as he continually struggled to re-construct his own sense of agency and authority. Only his level of activity kept him from the brink of severe depression. A boat loosely moored in violent waters, he found anchors in Paris and Rouen with visits to Joby and Gabrielle, both of whom offered a comforting ear and unfailing interest in his activities and concerns. A third anchor tied him to Césaire, now widely published in France, whose physical distance in no way diminished his force of influence over Fanon. Fanon's writings in this period draw heavily from Césaire, at times revealing outright imitation, and clearly exhibiting a writer struggling to discover his own voice under the din of a powerful and overwhelming literary presence that cannot be put out of mind.

As he neared the end of his medical school training and began to consider topics for a dissertation, he decided to assemble this collection of highly personal and penetrating essays and speeches into a single monograph for his thesis, which he titled, *Essay for the Disalienation of the Black*. Upon reading the first version, Joby suggested that he was too modest in the title, and offered a revised title, *Essay for the Disalienation of the Black and the White*. Fanon offered it to the medical faculty as a "clinical study," but received discouraging feedback. Their idea of a clinical study did not entail observing one's own subjective conscious reactions and extrapolating these to a generalized pathology, and furthermore Fanon's ideas of racial psychology were far too radical to be appreciated by a standard psychiatric faculty in 1950. At first angry and disappointed, he decided to revise the thesis into a book, submitted it to a publisher, and then chose a more conservative topic for his thesis.

The year 1951 progressed, and Fanon became more seriously involved in a relationship with Josie Dublé, a friend from Lyon he had met during the war and with whom he now felt closer than ever. She was a highly intelligent and strikingly attractive woman with long, black hair and golden skin. In both looks and personality she was nearly as intense as he was. The two enjoyed reading a great deal, and through their discussions they influenced and challenged each other intellectually. More importantly, she had offered him much emotional support over these recent turbulent years, and was understanding and tolerant given Fanon's complex character. As an added bonus, while Fanon could not stand to physically write or type, she was willing and happy to take dictation for his numerous writing projects.

By November Fanon had submitted a new, more conventional medical thesis entitled, *Troubles mentaux et syndromes psychiatriques dans l'hérédo-dégénération-spino-cérébelleuse. Un cas de maladie de Friedreich avec délire de possession.* On the inside cover he dedicated the thesis to his belated father, to his mother, and to his brothers and sisters. He singled out Joby in particular, and offered him a quotation from Nietzsche: "I only speak of living things, and I don't represent mental processes." One may be tempted to argue that the thesis fails on this promise, as its seventy-five pages contain a highly scholarly analysis of psychological problems associated with a particular neurological disease, and at first blush bears a dryness that is typical of medical case histories. But in fact the thesis provides interesting insights into the development of Fanon's individualized, cultural approach to psychotherapy that emphasizes the importance of a patient's worldview above any isolated mental process.

He begins by providing an insightful critique of psychological theories about genetics that reduce the patient's psyche to a simplified "roadmap" of medical psychopathology. Turning then to anthropology, Fanon invokes the thought of Lucien Lévy-Bruhl, whose observations of "primitive" mentalities in non-Western cultures drew him to emphasize the overwhelming prevalence of a law of "participation" in thought and worldview across cultures, whereby the Western emphasis on individualism is supplanted by belief in an all-encompassing essence of consciousness that permeates all living and nonliving things. Hence all objects, in all observable forms—whether of earth, liquid, gas or fire—participate with one another at the deepest, most personal level, such that a person can never be separated or abstracted from its environment. What may seem to be illogical assumptions and superstitions to a Western observer in fact reflect a deeply engrained ethical and spiritual code that places the individual in the context of an overarching participatory symbolic universe. A man is at once himself, and all others around him. He is the land, the air, the animals, and the culture, and these entities are inseparable.

In the context of Fanon's developing theory of human psychology, his attention to Lévy-Bruhl's law of participation reveals an early understanding of and sympathy for the patient's cultural worldview above and beyond any medical theory. The task of the psychiatrist, then, becomes not simply to interview the patient and then thumb through a book to uncover the diagnosis and solution, but to make an effort to "reach" the patient through the patient's own symbols and belief systems. Rather than focusing on symptoms, the approach focuses on the patient, or even *beyond* the patient, as the psychiatrist struggles to uncover those cultural "participations" at work in the patient's psyche. Before subscribing to any doctrine, the task of the doctor is to learn the doctrine of the patient. Fanon pragmatically applied this approach to everyday medical practice in an article submitted to *Esprit*, on the "North African Syndrome," where he severely criticized the stereotyped assumptions made about North African patients by European doctors, and called for recognition of fundamental cultural biases that required North African immigrants to adopt their style of "being a patient" to an alienating European model. His optimism for a better system—even a colonial one—comes through clearly:

> This means that there is work to be done over there, human work . . . It means that over the whole territory of the French nation . . . there are tears to be wiped away, inhuman attitudes to be fought, condescending ways of speech to be ruled out, men to be humanized.

These developments in Fanon's psychological thought provide equal insight into his spiritual development. While his first book—which would be published by Seuil as *Black Skin, White Masks* in the following year—focused on existential introspections of an individual struggling with himself and his own subjective responsibility, his medical thesis reveals a man with a much broader sense of himself as an individual partaking in a larger, cultural context of universal responsibility and collective involvement. As an extension of beliefs he had long held before this time, Lévy-Bruhl's insights on the law of participation were easily integrated into Fanon's longstanding conviction that he was responsible not only for himself, but for the whole of his surrounding culture, and, indeed, all of humanity. As if envisioning himself the very tool of Hegel's all-encompassing consciousness of *Weltgeist*, Fanon became more and more extended into an abstracted yet expanding and welcoming world. Perhaps in reaction to the culture that had so readily rejected and isolated him from participation among its own provincial recesses, Fanon developed an even stronger ideological conviction that he participated in something larger and greater, a human essence that transcended all insularity and positioned him in the center of a great, all-inclusive universe of psyche.

Fanon's medical thesis was defended before five professors from the medical faculty in late November. Though the thesis was thoroughly researched and Fanon had become a compelling speaker, two professors listened skeptically and then proceeded to question him at length on some of the details. This was probably typical of any thesis committee, but Fanon became flustered by their criticisms and refused to accept them, retorting with a barrage of statistics and facts concerning the syndrome discussed in his study. After two hours of heated debate, the skeptics at last relented, requiring only that he make a couple small changes before they accepted his work.

Several weeks later, after completing a course of supervised psychotherapy at the Hôpital de Saint-Ylie outside Lyon, Fanon traveled to Paris to present Joby with a final copy of his thesis. He had other news as well: a publisher in Paris had accepted his first book for publication. Since he was virtually unknown outside of Lyon, his next task was to find someone with a respected name to write a preface to the book, and his first choice was Francis Jeanson—a leftist philosophy professor, contributing editor for Sartre's journal *Les Temps Modernes*, and one of Sartre's close associates. Aside from his appeal of being associated with

Sartre's inner circle, Jeanson's political stance of national responsibility offered a perfect complement to Fanon's treatise. Fanon's book even quotes Jeanson's view of nationalized racism in France: "Every citizen of a nation is responsible for the actions committed in the name of that nation."

Shortly after sending Jeanson a copy of the manuscript with a letter asking him to consider writing a preface, Fanon was contacted by Jeanson's office and informed that Jeanson wished to meet him. The day of their appointment, Fanon approached Jeanson's office with some trepidation, as he had read Jeanson's reviews and knew him as a harsh critic. In fact, Jeanson was about to publish a devastating review of Camus' *The Rebel* that would lead to the end of any friendship between Camus and Sartre. But when it came to assessing Fanon's book, Jeanson was far from harsh. He was thrilled by the work, and, as Jeanson relayed it, "Having found his manuscript exceptionally interesting, I committed the error of telling him so."

To Jeanson's surprise, Fanon blazed with indignant anger. Fanon stood up and rebuked, "You mean, for a *Negro*, it isn't so bad!"

This was not at all what Jeanson had meant. Not being one to waste time in his relations with others, Jeanson showed Fanon to the door and communicated his own feelings with a fair amount of good-humored drama. Jeanson's honest response at once put Fanon at ease, for he realized this was a man who would say nothing if it was not straightforward. Given the overwhelming sensitivity from which Fanon often suffered, such open sincerity was essential in his friendships. The two became friends, and Jeanson offered him a number of editorial suggestions—which went mostly unheeded by Fanon. In response to a suggestion Jeanson made that he further clarify one of the phrases in the book, Fanon replied, "I cannot explain that phrase more fully. I try, when I write such things, to touch the nerves of my reader . . . That is to say, irrationally—almost sensually."

And the more Jeanson learned about Fanon, the more he understood what these words meant.

February in Martinique is Carnival season, when the islanders costume themselves in flamboyant and checkered attire of Madras cotton and spill to the streets in dance and revelry. Coming to the end of several years of hard work and estrangement in far away cities, both Frantz and Joby were low on finances but high in spirit on their return home. For Frantz the return was a triumphant one, with much news to tell: at age twenty-six, he had earned a degree in psychiatry, he was about to publish his first book, and the February issue of *Esprit*—one of France's most popular monthlies—carried his article among its pages. He brought back copies of his thesis and presented them to his mother and his brother Félix. On the cover of Félix's copy he offered a dedication with some additional references from Nietzsche:

> I have a horror of weaknesses—I understand them, but I do not like them.
>
> I do not agree with those who think it possible to live life at an easy pace. I don't want this. I don't think you do either . . .

The quotes he chose to represent his sentiments are telling of the great value he now placed on notions of strength, and of the resentment he harbored toward weakness and inactivity—especially his own. Perhaps as an effort to suppress his haunting feelings of sensitivity and vulnerability, there was something in him that needed to remain strong at all times, and that needed to keep moving, thinking, and working.

In Martinique this was difficult, as the island he once considered home had, in his absence, become stranger and more alien to him. In truth his old city and his old companions had not changed much; it was he who had changed, and changed a great deal. He found it more difficult to relate to people and their concerns; and even when he could, he found that the islanders remained curiously distant from him. His language and mannerisms had become less like those of the island bourgeoisie and more like those of a French intellectual. Even taking a pleasant stroll along the *Savane* in the evening hours and making trivial conversation with passersby could be an alienating experience that reinforced how different he had become. A regrettable remark such as, "It was not my good fortune, when in France, to observe mounted policemen" earned only snickers when he turned to walk on. Having returned from a long stay in France, he was now of that venerated and resented caste, as Césaire had become on his return; and like Césaire, he would learn that this echelon could be lonely and difficult.

Still, he was uncertain as to where his future might take him, and Europe remained no less alienating than his former homeland. To earn some money, he rented an office in Vauclin in the south of the island and saw patients as a general practitioner. Many patients were exceedingly poor and lacked basic needs— as well as the means of self-sustenance by which to maintain a healthy esteem—and Fanon's services were frequently offered without charge. In the small amount of spare time the practice allowed him, he continued to read extensively and kept up with developments in psychiatry journals. From these and from his observations regarding the relationship between health, psychology, and the dispossessed economy around him, he continued to revise and advance his own theories about the political and social origins of many ailments.

Aside from these private undertakings, the intellectual life on the island was stagnant. In his current position, it would be difficult to advance the widespread social changes that could affect any of these problems. And furthermore, the entirety of that role in Martinique—the role of the island intellectual, the role of the social reformist, the role of the political advocate for a downtrodden people—was filled by the immense figure named Césaire, from whose shadow Fanon now needed to withdraw. Martinique had become Césaire's territory, and Fanon, while continuing to respect Césaire a great deal, needed to tread his own path, and needed to do it in a field of his own.

That summer he closed his office in Vauclin, said good-bye to his mother and siblings, and boarded a ship back to France. He never returned to Martinique again.

The psychiatric hospital at Blida-Joinville.
(Algerian National Press and Information Documentation Center)

7

Liberator of Minds

> Who is enslaved,
> if not the man enslaved by his own mind?
> —*Karl Jaspers*

IN FRANCE THERE WERE A number of institutions where Fanon could put his social theories of psychology into practice. One psychiatrist at Saint-Alban was widely known for his radical approaches to the practice of psychiatry, a small and lively man from Barcelona named François Tosquelles, exiled in France after the Spanish Civil War due to his outspoken political convictions. The methods of Tosquelles were radical for their time, and were summed under the title of *thérapeutique institutionnelle*, or "communal therapy," which described a set of techniques designed to reacquaint the patient with society by providing a supportive model of the community within the hospital itself. Tosquelles vehemently opposed the institutional atmosphere that was typical of psychiatry at that time, and replaced the barren and isolating psychiatric ward with a colorful and integrative community. Patients were given work responsibilities commensurate with their level of functioning, and spent most of their time in groups or other socially-encouraging activities. Most importantly, they were incited to adopt a role within the context of this miniaturized society—which Tosquelles considered to be a critical step on the path to psychological wellness. This setting, combined with prescriptions of barbiturates and moderate electroshock therapy, Tosquelles named the "Bini method." For mentally ill patients in 1952, it was, above all, a method of liberation.

Thus it is hardly surprising that this would be the doctor Fanon sought to work with, and who would soon become his mentor in the field of psychiatry. In the late summer Fanon began a residency with Tosquelles at the Hôpital de Saint-Alban in the southern French countryside of Lozère near the town of Mende. Fanon was one of the most intelligent, enthusiastic and hard-working residents Tosquelles had ever known, and he seemed limitless in his energy and in his knowledge of psychological, social, and philosophical theory. Similar in many ways, both men shared a love of life and all things intellectual. But at times Tosquelles felt that Fanon was overly occupied with proving himself when Tosquelles was already sufficiently impressed. He made appeals to Fanon to slow down and spend more time contemplating the details of his findings. But to Fanon, contemplation was synonymous with working, writing, and interacting. Thought, as always, meant action.

In many ways, what Tosquelles put into practice was the direct embodiment of what Fanon had already written about in theory. Tosquelles also was influenced by social and anthropological ideas, and argued that psychiatry must assume an "anthropological" view of mental health that would integrate observations on the patient's biology, sociology and history in addition to standard psychological considerations. Tosquelles challenged both doctors and staff to reassess their roles and assumptions in interactions with patients, breaking down the customary distance between patients and staff, and encouraging more interpersonally-involved forms of therapy. Nurses were encouraged to actively participate as much as possible, abandoning their traditional roles as adult babysitters in favor of fostering an integrated community in which each person, whether staff or patient, carried a sense of purpose and responsibility.

Highly sensitive to the need for security and structure among the mentally-ill, Tosquelles rigorously organized the hospital into "quarters" that were in turn broken down into smaller, well-supervised groups of ten to twelve patients who lived and worked together in a kind of surrogate family. He taught his staff to pay attention to every detail, with two or three doctors assigned to each patient, and no detail went unnoticed by Tosquelles, who made constant, tiny revisions in attempts to improve the system. Furthermore, staff were entreated to include the patients in their meetings, so that patients would become participants in their own therapies and gain insight into their own illness, and not remain oblivious objects of observation.

In October of 1952 Frantz Fanon and Josie Dublé were married, and Josie continued her nascent work as a journalist while Frantz proceeded with his residency at Saint-Alban. In addition to the extraordinary efforts he put into working at the hospital, Fanon maintained many outside interests, reading voraciously and writing notes and ideas for new articles and books. He had developed an interest in Trotsky's writings, and asked Manville, now a card-carrying member of the Communist party, to bring him a copy of the proceedings of the Fourth International Congress of the Communist party, also attended by Césaire.

Fanon was also fascinated by the racial situation in the United States, and he became enthralled by the author Richard Wright. After obtaining Wright's home address from Alioune Diop—who had become Fanon's friend and correspondent through his association with Césaire, and who had published Wright in *Présence Africaine*—Fanon penned a humble letter to

Wright from his desk at Saint-Alban in the first week of 1953. He praised Wright highly and claimed to be at work on a study of "the luminous scope" of Wright's works, specifying what he had read and asking Wright to enlighten him on any titles he had missed. By now Fanon had honed an art of writing letters to establish contact with important people who inspired him, and the letter served equally to introduce his own name to Wright. In the final paragraph he wrote, "My name must be unknown to you—I wrote an essay, *Black Skin, White Masks* . . . where I endeavored to demonstrate the systematic ignorances of Whites and Blacks." The grace of his manner ensured that Wright would remember him when they met three years later. In fact Fanon's intended study was not solely on Wright, but on the entire racial predicament in the United States at that time, which Fanon believed to presage a coming evolution in racial relations worldwide.

This study—and undoubtedly countless others—would never come to fruition. Fanon's work at the hospital consumed most of his time, and he and another resident published one clinical study during that year, while preparing four additional studies that would be presented with Doctor Tosquelles and his colleagues at a conference in Pau that coming summer. Looming over his daily efforts was also anticipation of the last exam he would take in the summer, the *Médicat des hôpitaux psychiatriques*, which determined with all finality whether he was sufficiently qualified to practice as a licensed psychiatrist. In the late spring he took a break from his research at the hospital and buried himself in study materials, reviewing his notes from medical school and rereading textbooks and articles. Out of nearly two hundred doctors taking the exam that year, less than one third were expected to make high enough marks on the exam to continue as psychiatrists. The exam consisted of several days' worth of written examinations in topics as diverse as pathology, neurology, and forensic medicine. Even if these tests were corrected to the satisfaction of the examiners, one still faced the exacting oral portion of the exam, which in psychiatry entailed an extensive assessment and diagnosis of several patients selected and carefully supervised by seven senior examiners wearing magisterial robes.

For Frantz, the oral exam took place on Bastille Day in the heat of July in Paris. Accompanied by Josie, they met Joby on their arrival to the jubilant city and the three proceeded to the Sainte Anne Psychiatric Hospital, where the afternoon exam would be administered. Joby and Josie waited patiently in the reception room. Inside, they could hear Frantz's determined voice arguing over theory with his oral examiners. After some time the voices reached a kind of conclusion, and Fanon was required to make examinations of several psychiatric patients that his examiners had specially selected. One of the patients was a French woman, and as Fanon approached her she stood up and cried out, "Get this Black away from me!" Frantz could hardly doubt that this was part of the test—*his test*, at any rate—and that the examiners had selected this patient for him for just this reason. But Fanon had handled similar situations before, and had even come to expect them, and so proceeded with the examination, politely asking questions of the woman in spite of her ongoing protests. As the evening wore on the exam did not become any less like a circus, and the spectacular atmosphere was only augmented when Bastille Day fireworks began to explode outside the window. As Josie and Joby waited patiently and listened, one of the candidates came out into the waiting room and witnessed their pained expressions.

"Do you know that doctor who is taking his exam now?" he asked them.

"Yes," Joby replied. "He's my brother."

The candidate's burst of laughter put them at tentative ease.

"Oh, he's fantastic!" the man exclaimed, and pointed to the fiery scene out the window. "Fireworks on the outside! . . ." he remarked, and then gesturing back toward the room from where he had come and from where the wrangle of Fanon's examination still echoed, he declared, "Fireworks on the inside!"

Passing the Médicat assured Fanon of the esteemed position of *chef de service* at any psychiatric institution in France with an open post. His first offer was to assume the directorship of a hospital in Martinique, but Fanon refused on the basis that it had no facilities for psychiatric care or research. Furthermore, the idea of returning to Martinique failed to carry much appeal. He was not enthused about the idea of staying in France, and wrote to Césaire's longtime friend and fellow poet Léopold Senghor, now the president of Senegal, to see if he could obtain a post there. Senghor failed to respond, but Fanon still wished to get out of France. His true aspiration was to work in some remote and impoverished location, but not so remote as to be entirely lacking in facilities.

After attending the conference at Pau that spanned the third week in July, Fanon made a lukewarm acceptance to an offer at Pontorson, a small town near the coast of the English Channel between Normandy and Brittany, not far from the famed castle at Mont Saint Michel. A quiet and serene setting, from the gray stone hospital one heard the calm rush of the Couesnon river as it coursed its way to the channel through the peaceful French marshes. The hospital was surrounded by beautiful lawns and gardens, the staff was friendly, the patients were manageable, and there was very little work to do. For many, it was heaven. For Fanon, it was hell. He tried to keep himself busy, but in truth he was utterly bored. At Pontorson there were certainly sick patients to tend to, but they were not the types of patients Fanon

Ahmed Ben Bella, leader
of the Algerian Revolution.
(Algerian National Press
and Information Documentation Center)

could really feel enthusiastic about. The whole situation had a congenial bourgeois quality to it that turned his stomach. There were no battles to fight, and no authorities to challenge. After several months of excruciating ennui, he told his brother Joby about his dissatisfaction with the job. "I do not want to stay here," he confessed. "In France there are enough psychiatrists to cure all the patients in France. I want to go to Africa . . . I want to go to a country under domination to cure the sick."

He would soon get his wish. In mid-October he heard of a position available at a hospital in the French colony of Algeria, and immediately applied for the job. He had become fascinated with Algeria during his stay there in the military, and it seemed just the kind of place where he could practice psychiatry and work on social and political theory at the same time. Within a few weeks the Algerian hospital at Blida-Joinville had accepted him, and Frantz and Josie were again packing their belongings, having lived at Pontorson for only a few months, to begin a new life in Algeria.

The social climate in Algeria when the Fanons arrived in late November of 1953 was one with which Frantz was readily familiar: a country colonized by France, where the arable land and the economy were controlled by European minority. Though the majority of the indigenous Muslim population was extremely poor, illiterate, and relegated to a status of near-invisibility in the eyes of most European colonists, a century's worth of "assimilation" policy had created an educated middle class of Algerians who had made various attempts to organize in the hope of bettering the plight of downtrodden Algerian Arabs. But Algeria was much closer to France than Martinique, and France depended heavily upon Algerian resources like coal and iron, and also relied upon Algeria as a primary consumer of French products. By the end of the Second World War, French colonial policy considered Algeria to be nothing less than the extension of France's borders across the Mediterranean, and Algerian nationalist yearnings prompted the project of assimilation to be intensified under the guise of concessions to Algerian demands. Such concessions were at first made with little sincerity—Algerian men were granted the right to vote, but elections were promptly rigged—and when the emergence of a well-organized and armed Algerian revolutionary force seized colonial attentions in November of 1954, that sincerity was offered too late.

A year earlier, the Fanons traveled to an Algeria that had yet to become overrun with political strife, though its cauldron had begun to seethe beneath a tepid surface. Arriving at the largest psychiatric hospital in Algeria, Blida-Joinville lay some thirty miles southwest of Algiers in the farm-riddled countryside at the base of the Atlas mountains. The hospital complex encompassed a series of white stone buildings and gardens with walkways, enclosed by a high stone wall that isolated the hospital oasis from surrounding fields of wheat and grain. Isolation was a prevailing theme throughout the complex, which carefully segregated its two thousand patients into European "settlers" and the remaining Algerian "natives." The two groups were kept separate with Europeans receiving better treatment, which was still sadly inadequate given only six psychiatrists and a handful of nurses and interns to supervise the entire complex. The wards themselves remained closed and isolated, and patients were not allowed to leave their small and dingy dormitories, except for brief supervised periods in the exercise yard. The complex's extensive and beautiful gardens were reserved for staff. While a few staff members believed the situation could be improved, the hospital director, Monsieur Kriff, exhibited more interest in his own busy social life than in bettering conditions at the hospital, and made only brief and indifferent appearances there. Hence it was the task of poorly trained and unsupervised interns and nurses to handle everyday problems, which were frequently dealt with by isolation and locked doors.

A legend exists that on the day Frantz Fanon first surveyed his ward at Blida-Joinville, he found patients chained to their beds, struggling merely to move, and that he at once ordered his staff to remove the chains, to allow the patients to walk freely, and never to restrain them again. The legend has since been refuted by some of Fanon's closest colleagues whose presence at Blida preceded Fanon's, and who insist there were never any chains. But, they hasten to add, Fanon wasted no time in instituting changes on the ward that were equally, if not more, radical; and that were equally, if not more, liberating. Many patients were indeed straight-jacketed, and when Fanon's orders to nurses to remove the jackets were answered with looks of confusion and disbelief, his unequivocal reiteration of the command inspired a hurried compliance. As his staff gathered in the doorway to witness the spectacle this new doctor was instigating, Fanon inquired if they did not have any duties to attend to. Some withdrew, but many remained, and Fanon ignored the onlookers as he moved from patient to patient, introducing himself with a calm and earnest demeanor, informing each that he would be available for consultation at any hour.

Fanon's second radical action was to utterly abolish the prevalent distinction between European and "native." Even the mere reference to a patient as one or the other was forbidden. The wards would now be totally integrated, and there would be no difference in the treatment offered to any patient on the basis of ethnicity, wealth or background. Furthermore, the wards were now considered open, and any patient who did not exhibit violent behavior was free to enter and leave the main wards at will, and the hospital grounds with its walkways and gardens would be open to them as much as to anyone else. As for lower-functioning patients on the closed wards, they were admitted outside and onto the open wards for supervised activities on a regular and scheduled basis. As with the rigid structure at Saint-Alban, all sections would be carefully supervised by interns and nurses, who in turn reported to Fanon. Their goal was to graduate patients from lower-functioning sections to higher ones, and eventually out of the hospital. This was a radical concept to the staff, as they regarded most inmates as patients for life.

Fanon sought neither to obtain permission from nor to inform Director Kriff of the changes he was instituting, and with the latter's frequent absence some time passed before he would notice anything different. One afternoon Kriff passed through the main ward and sensed an eerie emptiness as he crossed to his office. A few minutes later, he glanced out the window and witnessed a scene he could not believe: there in the courtyard were some two dozen patients, escaped from the ward and running up and down the yard in psychopathic mania. He immediately called the hospital *gendarmes*, a squad of which accompanied him down to the courtyard a few moments later. There he found Fanon, stripped to his undershirt and standing in the center of the grassy yard with a sheepish band of perspiring patients.

"What on earth is going on here?" Kriff demanded.

Fanon stared at him, bewildered. "What's going on, Monsieur Director? What's going on? We're playing soccer. Can't you see? What's the problem?"

Director Kriff, after a moment of hesitation, at last admitted that there was no problem, that he had been caught off guard by the unexpected activity, and would Fanon mind to please inform him in advance the next time he planned to remove patients from the confines of the ward.

This was exactly what Fanon would not do, for in his eyes

there were only two types of staff members at the hospital: those who supported his efforts, and those who did not. And as far as Fanon was concerned, Director Kriff proved himself among the latter. A majority of the staff fell into this category as well, including all but one of the other psychiatrists, who came to refer to Fanon merely as "the Black doctor." Among his supporters was a single *chef de service*, a young French psychiatrist named Doctor Lacaton who had recognized the need for change before Fanon's arrival but required some encouragement, and a couple of interns named Sanchez and Azoulay. For the most part, Fanon's major supporters were found among the Muslim male nurses, who began to pitch in with a renewed enthusiasm, and who were in turn awarded greater responsibilities and a more purposeful view of their daily activities. But as much as they admired him, the staff also came swiftly to fear him, becoming well acquainted with Fanon's explosive temper and his impatience with negligence or idleness.

Aided by a handful of nurses, three interns, and Doctor Lacaton, Fanon set about the creation of a new community. As with the system at Saint-Alban, Fanon divided the wards into small groups that shared working and living responsibilities. Group therapy became an everyday event, and patients received individualized consultations on a regular basis. Between scheduled group sessions, Fanon set any able-bodied patient to work on some project or another, providing work therapy in the guise of gardening or painting or making general improvements to the dormitories. In reward for these efforts, patients were then thrown parties or provided with entertainments previously unavailable to them. Just as Tosquelles had done, Fanon sought to recreate a model of the outside community within the ward: he arranged some furniture into a café, dragged an unused projector and some chairs into a room to fashion a small cinema, and used the hospital mimeograph to start a weekly newspaper, *Notre Journal*, which any patient could read or contribute to (though most of the writing was done by Doctors Fanon and Lacaton). Many patients readily responded, and the café and cinema became populated with patients who had remained socially isolated only six months before. The newspaper, admittedly, failed to attract a significant readership—let alone any additional writers—but Fanon continued to produce it nonetheless.

While the new system was a vast success in many ways, it proved a complete failure in others. Fanon's efforts did inspire a marked improvement in functioning for a significant number of patients, many of whom managed to graduate from one level of supervision to the next, and eventually were released from the hospital to return to their families and former homes. But an equally significant number of patients did not respond, and the difference between these two groups was painfully obvious: it was the Europeans who were thriving, and the native Algerians who would not progress. This was especially frustrating and perplexing to Fanon, who had made every effort to ensure that all patients were treated similarly, and that no person suffered for treatment on account of ethnicity. Still, the discharge rates spoke for themselves, and Fanon scowled at repeated comments from his fellow *chefs de service* inquiring as to what more he had expected; after all these were only Arabs—lazy, immoral, good-for-nothing Arabs, and of course his efforts would not reach them, for there was nothing in them to reach.

Even the more enthusiastic nurses lost some of their enthusiasm when it came to dealing with Algerian patients. They would not attend or cooperate in groups, they refused to participate in scheduled activities, and they seemed vastly unenthused by any of the activities so readily adopted by European patients.

One of the nurses claimed that Fanon simply did not understand the Algerians, but, "When you've been working with them for fifteen years like us, you'll understand. . . ." Fanon, however, would not be discouraged, and worked on the problem with an unstoppable ardor. He organized meetings with the Algerian patients to try to get at the root of the matter, but his inquiries were met with apathy or even open hostility. This he could not bear, and he constantly discussed the problem with his interns, noting every detail in how the two types of patients were treated, hoping to discover a significant difference.

In keeping with his unfailing attention to language, the first difference he noted between the two groups was how they were spoken to. Because most of the Algerians did not speak French, nurses were required as interpreters during therapy sessions, and Fanon surmised that the additional distance created by this fact hindered the therapeutic relationship. To overcome the problem, he began learning Arabic himself. But furthermore, was French not also the language of the oppressing colonizer? For an Algerian Muslim, was French not the language of regulations and proscriptions, of senseless authority and self-serving laws and condescending bureaucracy? Ideas began to take shape, and he soon came to the realization that his attempt at sociotherapy failed among the Algerians not because they were treated differently from Europeans, but because they were treated the *same* as Europeans.

Here were two vastly different cultures, with two vastly different perspectives on the nature of society, and Fanon knew these facts well from his own previous writings and his own understanding of cultural participation. But his labors thus far had amounted at bottom to his own project of "assimilation"—an effort to erase one culture by imposing a different one. For most Algerians a cinema was an unheard-of social pastime, and his newspaper was worthless to an illiterate farmer. The holidays celebrated at the hospital were not Muslim holidays, and any café that allowed men and women to socialize freely with one another was anathema to Muslim beliefs. But if a healthy Algerian personality was going to be reconstructed from a sick one, it had to be reconstructed within the context of an Algerian culture. Fanon at once arranged a study, analyzing every difference he could ascertain between the two cultures, and received encouraging results. When the Algerian patients were prompted to concentrate on activities more central to their cultural values—activities that focused on family relations, storytelling, traditional Arabic games, and tending to their own plots of land in the garden—Fanon and his colleagues witnessed drastic changes in attitude and behavior, and marked their efforts a success. Fanon published his first paper from Blida on the project later that year.

Most of Fanon's colleagues at Blida-Joinville, however, cared little about his successes or his failures, and viewed him as irascible and slightly delirious, and a thorn in their collective side. His radical changes had upset a longstanding status quo, and he was deeply resented for it. Fanon resented them right back, and did nothing to smooth the feathers he so frequently ruffled. Staff meetings often culminated in Fanon making belligerent but painfully accurate remarks and criticizing the efforts of the other doctors, questioning their dedication and condemning the administration of the hospital for its lack of support.

Even his own staff had a difficult time with him, viewing him as oversensitive and critical. His detached and scientific attitude, while exhibiting his total dedication to his work, helped little to improve his relations with others. They knew he worked almost constantly, sleeping only four or five hours a night, and working six or seven days a week. At four in the morning he would appear on the ward to review notes of nurses, or he would be found in his office, writing or reading under the dim light of a desk lamp. At times he expected a similar commitment from his staff, which they were not always ready to give. His immense self-confidence could be impressive and inspiring, but sometimes he was too confident, and would absolutely refuse to compromise on even minor issues. An ignorant question or remark incited a flash in his eyes as he answered with vitriolic ridicule. He knew just where to find people's weaknesses, though they felt incapable of returning criticisms to him outright, as he exhibited an excessive sensitivity at being the only black doctor in the hospital, and he readily attributed conflicts to this incontrovertible fact.

Yet when Fanon shined, the light filled every open mind. His power of speech was captivating, and his analyses of problems and theories were brilliant and inspirational. He could stand and expound on a subject for hours without becoming repetitive or dull, and he gave the impression of being able to hold every perspective in his mind at once, weaving them slowly into a complete and compelling picture of an object or situation. He played out the roles of people he described, and his voice and facial expressions constantly changed as he moved from one emotion to another, from one idea to the next. Though perfectly comfortable in the abstract, when speaking with interns and nurses he consistently shaped theoretical ideas into concrete and personal examples from his own life that seemed to arise from some wellspring of profound inner-awareness. Lecturing at the local *lycée* from time to time, the normally listless group of students sat wide-eyed in their seats once Fanon began to speak, and one eighteen-year-old student found him so compelling that she applied to work with him as soon as she graduated.

Indeed, for all of the grief he gave them, for all of the love and hate they were made to feel for him, the interns and nurses serving at Blida-Joinville knew without a doubt that Doctor Fanon was one person who truly and deeply cared about every detail at the institution. In a hospital once hollow with apathy, their choice was to stand in the fire, or to stand not at all.

Many preferred the fire.

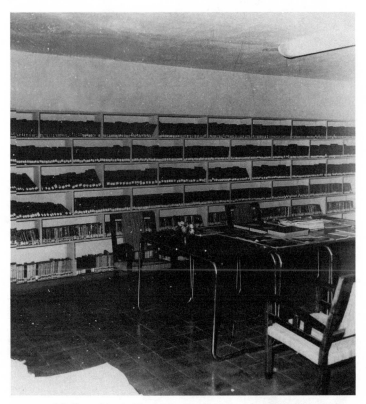

The psychiatric library inside the hospital at Blida-Joinville.
(Algerian National Press and Information Documentation Center)

Demonstrators in Algiers, 1958.
(© Bettmann/CORBIS)

8

Revolution

The master's tools will never dismantle the master's house.
—Audre Lorde

CAMUS ADROITLY CONDENSED the petty lives suffered by European colonists in Algeria in his description of their stunted passions: "Men and women devour each other quickly in what they call the act of love, or commit to a long mutual habitude. . . . for lack of time and reflection, one is well obliged to love without knowledge." Indeed this resolved unconsciousness, this hurried myopia, this benighted apathy as they carried cheeses from small shops to patios, would well serve any conscience seeking to blot out the violence one's very presence enacted, an aggression in the mere act of standing, while just at the outlands of vision stood destitute testimonies to the countless displaced forsaken.

Considering this necessary night they inhabited, it little surprises that a majority of colonists in Algeria found the events of the first of November in 1954—when a sudden and well-organized outbreak of ambushes, bombings, arsons, and general destruction aimed at police stations and municipal buildings swept the country—to come as an utter shock. Despite many indications, despite nationalist movements that had arisen and intensified over a hundred and fifty years of thoughtless oppression and discrimination, despite the bloody struggles against French colonialism that had gripped Morocco to the west and Tunisia to the east, Algeria had maintained a peaceful and smug façade. The thought of a coordinated, intelligent and uncompromising revolutionary force was nearly unthinkable, and the response of colonial might was immediate and brutal.

For Fanon, these events were not as surprising. For one, his vantage was that of a newcomer to the arena, an outsider, which allowed a widened breadth of perspective. But even more important, in only a year of service in the colony he had bent an earnest ear to voices that most would ignore through a lifetime, and in those voices he discerned cries of psyche that spoke of immense, unleashed power. It was a power he readily discerned, because it was a power he knew in himself. Thus to learn that the Algerian middle class had organized into a concerted revolutionary effort that would call itself the *Front de Libération Nationale*—the FLN—seemed to him a logical evolution. What he found more surprising was the reaction of the French, whom he had known to be ignorant, but had never known to achieve the degree of barbaric cruelty he would soon witness.

France, admittedly, was not in an enviable position. Following a century of rapid worldwide colonial expansion, the Second World War left France economically vulnerable, its resources spread thinly throughout the globe, and with the coming defeats in Indo-China, Morocco and Tunisia, it now witnessed a chain-reacting disintegration of its once-grand empire. Without its colonies, France would lose much of its clout in the international political arena. Algeria was the last straw, on which France absolutely refused to loosen its grip. In repeated efforts to abolish nationalist sentiments and to weaken rural support for the FLN, extreme measures of torture and terror were taken against rebels and random innocent civilians alike. On Fanon's end, this would first arise in direct orders from government superiors calling for heavy discrimination among the medical community. Medicines such as antibiotics and analgesics were to be distributed to Europeans only, and medical services to Algerians were considered absolutely secondary. It was the task of every doctor to report suspicious injuries or activities among Algerians to the colonial authorities. Fanon watched as an overwhelming majority of his medical colleagues followed such orders without question, in gross violation of Hippocratic ethics. He could conceive of only one response to such malevolence: to work directly against it, providing a haven against discrimination, and offering medical services where they were otherwise refused.

Only a few months into these events Fanon was struck by a greater, more personal tragedy. In the first days of February a telegram arrived. It read merely, "Gabrielle deceased." Frantz was beside himself with disbelief. He gripped the telegram in his hand and read it over and over, attempting to get through to Martinique or Paris by telephone to obtain some indication that the words were not true, that the telegram was in gross error. But a forthcoming letter from Joby confirmed his worst fear. In the course of childbirth an accident had occurred, and his beloved sister was dead. In a grief-stricken letter to his mother he expressed his continued incapacity to fully accept the news, calling the death "absurd, illogical, ludicrous, inexplicable." He repeatedly emphasized the strength of will Gabrielle exhibited in life, and declared that only the most unfair struggle could have defeated her. Equally bewildered by his own incapacity to accept the news, he wrote, "Maybe the proximity of this Islamism is acting on me; what explanations satisfy the mind when they are of death?"

The blow could only be softened by the recent birth of his own son. Born to an uncertain world, the new child brought hope

Algeria, in Brief

The region now known as Algeria sustained two invasions by crusading Islamic Arabs in the seventh and eleventh centuries, whose proselytism converted most of the indigenous Berber population to the teachings of Islam. A third invasion in the sixteenth century brought the Berbers under rule of the Turks, and the Mediterranean shore of northern Africa—now Morocco, Algeria and Tunisia—became the westernmost outlands of the Ottoman Empire, known as the Maghreb (which for the Turks meant simply, "the West").

But this remote region of the empire soon succumbed to corsairs along the coast, and Algiers developed into a notorious nest for pirates of the Mediterranean, who raided European shipping and used European slaves to row their ships. The viciousness of marauders along the Barbary Coast lacked a word sufficient to describe it, and the pirate acts were simply dubbed "Barbarian," a word that came to speak for itself.

The French first attacked Algiers in 1683 in an attempt to subdue piracy, and in 1827 a quarrel over money culminated when the Dey of Algiers slapped the French consul with a fly whisk. Two years later, in an effort to distract the population from Charles X's growing unpopularity, the French invaded a small part of the coast. This maneuver did not prevent Charles X from losing power, and the French Army, left to its own devices, continued its conquest until the coast was entirely occupied.

The first group of European settlers in Algeria were an unwitting group of 400 Rhinelanders who left Le Havre in 1832, their minds and hearts set on a new life in America. However, their unscrupulous captain had other ideas, and rather than cross the perilous Atlantic he sailed out beyond sight of land, turned south, and deposited the settlers on the shore of Algeria, his passengers none the wiser until he had long sailed off. Forty years later came the German occupation of Alsace, when another 500 Alsatians fled their homes and settled in Algeria, this time on purpose. Algerian land was made freely available to French soldiers, and in 1873 the application of French property laws to Muslim land holdings made confiscation of the land from its previous owners an exceedingly easy undertaking.

to a couple whose lives were becoming increasingly complicated. For Josie, life in Blida was difficult and isolating. Though they lived in a pleasant house on the hospital grounds, with increased security and escalating tensions in the surrounding region made the hospital oasis more a remote and imprisoning island.

Beginning in April, Marcel Manville visited them regularly, having taken several defense cases in Algeria. He was one of a handful of French lawyers who would offer legal counsel to members of the FLN, and this brought him to Algeria with increasing frequency. Every occasion he came to Algiers, he found Fanon waiting for him at the airport, and Fanon insisted that he stay at their house in Blida, lending Manville their car to drive back and forth to the city. Between Algiers and Blida the police installed checkpoints in an attempt to curb rebel transport between Algiers and the mountain regions. One afternoon Fanon drove to the city to retrieve Manville from the airport, and on their return, when cars slowed as they neared a check-point, Fanon accelerated. They passed the first group of soldiers who watched them with cool astonishment. The next group leveled their rifles and stood poised against the oncoming vehicle. Fanon stomped the brakes, and a rifle muzzle struck the window. The soldier looked in at them.

"Ten more meters, and you would have been dead," he said.

A few minutes later, having displayed their papers, they drove on.

Though he readily disregarded the standing order not to treat suspected members of the FLN and had challenged local authorities by forbidding police to bring guns into the hospital and by insisting that the military reroute its jets from their path above the hospital, Fanon had little direct involvement in the revolutionary efforts until he met Pierre Chaulet, a young European surgeon who carried out his first secret operation on a wounded FLN rebel in May of 1955. Having made his ideological convictions clear, the FLN soon sent Chaulet to Blida to construct a network of supporters. After a long evening of dinner and conversation at the Fanon house, he invited Fanon to contribute anonymous writings to some FLN publications, and to make his services more directly available if he wished. Fanon readily assented. From this moment onward, the psychiatric hospital at Blida became increasingly reputed in FLN circles as a safe haven for recovering rebels. Beds were made available, and minor surgeries performed secretly by Fanon and his close associates.

With the war mounting in ferocity each month, the hospital received an increase in admissions, and disastrous problems were narrowly avoided. On one occasion an outpatient—a European policeman who conducted "interrogations" by way of continuous torture—came to Fanon haunted by hallucinatory screams he heard in the night. Screams had become a matter of expertise for the man, who could identify the use of a certain torture merely by the scream it induced. "A man who's had two blows from a fist and a baton behind the ear has a certain way of speaking, of screaming, of saying he's innocent. After he's been left two hours strung up by his wrists he has another kind of voice . . . above all it's after the electricity that it becomes really too much." One day as Fanon returned home for his appointment with the man he found his patient huddled under a tree in an attack of anxiety. While waiting for his therapy session to begin, the man had gone for a walk across the hospital grounds, and there stumbled upon an FLN rebel he had viciously tortured only some weeks before. Fanon gave the patient a sedative and sent him home after the therapy session. The torturer's victim, having faced again the demon of his madness, was later found in a toilet attempting to commit suicide.

Under increased pressure from work and from his mounting involvement with the FLN, Fanon allowed himself little time for enjoyment, except during visits from Manville in which he exposed a wistful nostalgia for his family, his old friends, and their old home. On the event of Manville's arrival Fanon would at once inquire about his brother Joby in Paris, and would insist that Manville describe everything they had done together and recount every conversation Manville could recall having passed between them. Manville's career allowed him to travel to Martinique with some frequency, and Fanon as eagerly inquired about these trips as well, again needing every detail. When they arrived at the house Fanon would break out his old 78rpm records of Stellio, father of the *Biguine marseillaise*, and call to Josie that tonight they simply *must* have marinated cod for dinner, much to the satisfaction of both men, even if the dish never tasted quite like they knew from the island.

Though Manville offered his services to members of the FLN in the legal arena, Fanon was continually prompting him to become more directly involved in the revolutionary effort. But Manville was reluctant to engage in any action that fell outside the law. He was not convinced of the necessity of the violent struggle to begin with, believing that legal action, negotiation, and the rule of law could eventually bring a peaceful settlement—even one that would bring Algeria the independence it sought. Fanon countered that France would never give up its colony without a violent struggle; the very actions of the French had already manifested this fact. The French wanted Algeria, and they wanted it badly enough to disregard every law and every ethic of humanity conceived by modern civilization. Manville's thoughts reflected those of many leftist intellectuals in France, with whom Fanon bitterly debated, and who called for French reconsideration of its claim on Algeria, but argued the violent struggle undertaken by the FLN was unnecessary. And though Manville did not see eye-to-eye with his friend on the matter, he did not fault him for his involvement, and admired Fanon's unwavering commitment to the liberation effort.

One night Manville slept soundly in the Fanon guestroom after a long discussion at dinner. In a nearby village, a band of young European men took up rifles and set out to inflict terror and looting on several small communities of Algerians camped at the outskirts of town. When they reached a camp at Cazouna, they roused twenty men from their beds, marched them in line to the edge of the camp, and opened fire until none were left standing. One of the twenty was a male nurse at Blida named Cabbiche, who amidst the blurred horror found presence of mind to throw himself to the ground before he was struck by the bullets. For an hour he lay quiet beneath the blood and carnage of his dying friends and relatives, and listened to songs bellowed by the killers as they reloaded their rifles and withdrew from the camp.

At dawn Manville awoke with a start to the decisive call of Fanon, whose urgent summons bid him to dress in a hurry and make haste to the hospital lounge. There he saw Cabbiche, his semblance that of an ambulant ghoul for all of the blood that drenched him. Fanon stood livid and trembling, his hand shaking as he lifted it in insistent indication.

"Here," his voice quivered, "is what the French do habitually in this country! And to think that some of my intellectual friends, who pretend to be humanists, reproach me for my total adherence to this struggle, for love and the dignity of humanity!"

After informing Manville of the night's events, Fanon entreated him to accompany Cabbiche back to the camp to urge the victimized families to file complaints against their attackers. Fanon knew in advance that he sent his friend on a futile mission, and

Manville would soon discover that not one of the surviving family members, amid their screams and sobs, would dare file a complaint for knowledge that the killers would return the next night and continue the slaughter. Feeling ashamed, Manville resolved to file the complaint himself, against Fanon's advisement. But at the town hall in Blida he was firmly dismissed by an official, who declared they did not handle records for Arabs.

Throughout 1956 the war grew progressively vulgar, and the population of Algeria separated along clear and vicious lines between nationalists and colonialists, dividing friends, neighbors and children. Another incident identical to the killings at Cazouna occurred in the nearby village of Rivet, this time with forty Algerians dragged from their beds and gunned down in the night, and not a single man was arrested for the murders. The name of Rivet became synonymous with the spreading brutality and injustice across the country. One boy of fourteen, who lost two family members in the Rivet killings and had overheard a remark that the French would kill all Algerians, enlisted the help of a younger Algerian boy to lure their European playmate into the hills where they took turns stabbing him to death with a knife, taking photos as they did so. The two boys readily admitted to the crime, and were brought to Fanon for evaluation.

When Fanon asked the younger boy about the act, the boy replied, "He was a good friend of ours . . . . One day we decided to kill him, because the Europeans want to kill all the Arabs. We can't kill big people. But we could kill ones like him, because he was the same age as us. We didn't know how to kill him. We wanted to throw him into a ditch, but he'd only have been hurt. So we got the knife from home and we killed him." When Fanon asked why they chose to kill a boy who was their friend, the boy explained, "Because he used to play with us. Another boy wouldn't have gone up the hill with us."

French soldiers in the Casbah, Algiers.
(Algerian National Press and Information Documentation Center)

A French soldier stands at the entrance to
the Casbah in Algiers, December 1960.
(AP/Worldwide Photos)

Though this may have seemed the logic of children, it too often reflected the logic of adults, condemned to an insane and uncontainable national predicament. In the eyes of a psychiatrist like Fanon, who viewed the human mind not as an isolated entity but as a field stretching out to encompass and participate in the surrounding culture, his cases revealed little beyond the dementia of an insane society. Diagnoses and therapeutic treatments were a pointless effort; the war, the institutionalized racism it upheld, and its attendant horrors explained much of what he witnessed, and to apply a cure and then send the patient back into the maddening world was an exercise in futility. Even innocent civilians could not step outside the hospital without fear of being randomly abducted by police vans that circled the towns and countryside, hoping to lay hands on a weak-willed informant.

Though the isolation of Fanon's ward helped keep his pro-nationalist activities out of sight of his fellow doctors, the ward developed a reputation as a nest of nationalist activity. One young European intern with nationalist sentiments, Charles Geronomi, came to work at Blida simply due to rumors surrounding the nationalist activities that went on there. These types of applicants were ushered into service on Fanon's ward, which by now was populated solely with nationalist interns and nurses. Geronomi was enlisted to help distribute *el Moudjahid*, the revolutionary publication of the FLN. Other doctors in the hospital had exhibited increasing resentment of Fanon, and their suspicions and anger about his activities mounted with each month. Through another *chef de service* or through some other informant, police learned that something was afoot at the Blida clinic, though their surprise raids and searches of the ward revealed nothing more than common hospital supplies and lunatic inmates (some had been taught exactly how to act in such situations). The police made random arrests of Fanon's nurses, a few of whom were taken away in vans and never returned. Why Fanon himself was not arrested and questioned is a matter of curiosity, though the authorities may have determined him to be external to the situation because of his status as a foreigner—and a black foreigner; his "invisibility" for once working in his favor. But a more likely explanation concerns Fanon's rising status among influential French intellectuals. His first book was now going into print in several foreign languages, and the last thing the police needed was a high-profile public review of their methods. Instead they went for Fanon's less public colleagues, including Doctor Lacaton.

Lacaton was removed from the hospital for several days, and taken to the interrogation room at police headquarters. The police were often more brutal with European suspects than they were with Algerians, viewing nationalist Europeans as traitors to their country as well as to their race. But police had to be careful about leaving evidence of their manipulations, as Europeans retained some means of legal recourse. They commenced with mere intimidation, leaving the victim to watch as they tortured several Algerians—selected at random from the street—to death. Subsequent efforts at persuasion included submerging the subject in a bathtub to the brink of drowning, administering painful enemas, and prolonged electrocution. When several days of such measures did not elicit any useful information, Doctor Lacaton's interrogators surmised that he was a nationalist sympathizer who was not directly related to the revolutionary effort, and they drove him to the pig farm of a European colonist and tossed him to a sty of angry pigs.

Lacaton returned to the hospital, packed a few of his belongings, and left for France. As it was only a matter of time before the police returned for their next victim, Geronomi, responsible for a young family, decided also to leave. Fanon remained, but now thwarted from aiding both the mentally ill and the nationalist effort, submitted a letter of resignation. Rather than resigning to his immediate superiors, the letter went directly to Robert Lacoste, the Governor General in Algiers, to whom he expressed his objections of conscience:

> . . . Madness is one of the means man has of losing his freedom. . . . the degree of alienation of the inhabitants of this country appears to be frightening.
>
> If psychiatry is the medical technique that aims to enable man no longer to be a stranger to his environment, I owe it to myself to affirm that the Arab, permanently an alien in his own country, lives in a state of absolute depersonalization. . . .

Though Fanon made a compelling humanitarian plea, Lacoste, an outright racist, was perhaps the last person who would heed or consider such a plea, having a reputation among French intellectuals for turning a stone deaf ear to any argument against France's claim over Algeria. One might just as well argue with an earthquake.

Even after swubmitting his resignation to the highest Algerian authority, Fanon remained at the hospital for several weeks in an effort to complete his unfinished projects. Then, at the turn of the new year in 1957, a letter of expulsion arrived, allowing him forty-eight hours to leave the country. At the same time that Fanon received his expulsion, the French in Algeria were welcoming General Raoul Salan—who had personally awarded Fanon the *Croix de guerre* twelve years before—as their new commander in the fight against the uncontrollable revolution. A day after receiving the letter of expulsion from Algeria, Frantz and Josie gathered their young son and their belongings and left both the house and the ward quiet and empty, for Fanon's nurses and interns had left as well.

The Fanons traveled first to Lyon to stay with Josie's parents for a short period, but then departed for Paris. Fanon was eager now to become more actively involved with the FLN, and wanted to do work at the revolutionary headquarters in Tunis. Tunisia had won its independence from France two years before, and now hosted the governing arm of the FLN. There were underground factions of the FLN in Paris as well, of which Francis Jeanson and his wife Colette were active participants, but Fanon wanted to return to North Africa to aid the struggle in the place where he could make the most difference. He appealed to Jeanson to find him passage to Tunisia and to help him make contact with the FLN, and Jeanson was glad to do so. Jeanson had long regarded Fanon as a trustworthy associate, and wanted to become closer friends with him, but found Fanon to be cool to his overtures, remaining distant and self-contained. Though Fanon was polite and dedicated to their mutual cause, he was quiet and brief with Jeanson, seeming to want to end conversations as quickly as possible. Jeanson concluded he was entirely preoccupied with returning to the struggle.

These primary weeks of 1957 in Paris would prove the last occasion that Frantz, Joby and Manville spent time together. By now the core members of the *Bande Raide* had become politically active professionals who had little time to spare. Frantz was concerned mostly with getting to Tunis, and determining what he would do when he got there. On learning of Frantz's intention to return to the FLN, Joby urged him to reconsider. "Frantz," he implored, "Don't go to Tunis. Stay in France." He could assist the revolution from Paris through his writings. At this time Paris hosted a contingency of pro-Algerian intellectuals, including Jeanson, Claude Lanzmann, Sartre and de Beauvoir, and an underground network of the FLN who worked to garner support and to route personnel and finances. But this was exactly why Frantz refused to stay. He did not wish to be a part of that group. He already had ideological disputes with many in the French left, and could not allow himself to sit comfortably in Paris while he knew others to be suffering. He countered Joby with the argument that there were already plenty of intellectuals in France. "France has Sartre," he said. "And France has Camus and Merleau-Ponty. They don't need me here. They need me in Tunis. And that's where I will go." Once again, he needed to forge his own path, and once again no argument could change his mind.

In early February Jeanson reported that Fanon's passage to Tunis had been arranged, and the FLN would oversee his transport. Within a few days Frantz said goodbye to his brother and friends, officially renounced his French citizenship, and departed again for the coast of North Africa.

9

The Struggle

Action isn't an explosion.
Action is a continual creation of a human order.

—*Frantz Fanon*

TUNIS PROVED TO BE OVERRUN with political activity. Hardly a
man on the street could be found who was not working with the
FLN, the CIA, the KGB or the *Deuxième Bureau*. And then
there were reporters. Given the recent independence of Tunisia
and Morocco, and given revolutionary uprisings in the Congo
and Angola, the fate of colonial Africa, and especially Algeria,
was now of primary interest to the international community.
The FLN itself occupied over one hundred and fifty buildings in
Tunis—its heavy financing allowed it to own some of the most
palatial buildings in the city—though Fanon worked in a small
and dingy stucco building that housed the Algerian press service,
shortly thereafter to become the Algerian Ministry of Information. Here Fanon took charge of the editorial office at the FLN
newspaper, *el Moudjahid*, the revolution's primary vehicle for
informing the public. While the newspaper had previously published mostly accounts of FLN victories in an effort to boost
public morale and support for the struggle, Fanon's arrival on
the staff marked the beginning of a change in content that would
increasingly include ideological discussions and political cri-

Roberto Holden, president of the Union of the Angolan Population,
and rebel leader in Angola.
(AP/Worldwide Photos)

tiques of international actions that related to the war; in short, *el Moudjahid* began to look more like Fanon's own writings.

Many of the articles in *el Moudjahid* arose directly from heated discussions among Fanon, his editor-in-chief Redha Malek, and Pierre Chaulet, who now worked in Tunis as the head of the FLN's *Centre de Documentation*. Chaulet and Malek were both central to the nationalist effort, and could supply any detail on the history of the struggle. Like Fanon and Chaulet, Malek was an electrified individual, who sat on the edge of his chair as he spoke. When the Ministry of Information was later formed, all three men reported to Mohammed Yazid, the Minister of Information, who led the group in a concerted effort to rally international support for the Algerian nationalist cause.

In addition to his work at *el Moudjahid*, Fanon continued to work as a doctor for the FLN health service, providing medical services and expertise as needed, and continued his psychiatric work at a hospital at Manouba under the name of Doctor Fares. This time Fanon made a fair effort to approach the director of the hospital, Ben Soltan, before instituting his widespread changes, presenting the director with a detailed plan that he proposed should be adopted by every *chef de service*. Soltan was in some ways the opposite of his former superior at Blida, in as much as he kept tabs on every detail of the hospital's activities, but he was also bureaucratic and parochial, sensitive about his authority, and, as a Tunisian educated in Europe, maintained a European view of class structure. When Soltan patently rejected Fanon's proposals on the premise that there was no money in the budget, Fanon responded that he would ask the Minister of Health to increase hospital funding. With his political connections, this was not difficult for Fanon to do, though Ben Soltan was furious at his audacity. From this day forward Soltan undertook a campaign to discredit Fanon, eventually presenting the

Minister of Health with an entire dossier of evidence that sup-posedly proved Doctor Fares to be a spy for Israel, who ought to be removed from his post and ejected from the country. By this point the Minister of Health had become well acquainted with Fanon's work, and dismissed the charge as ludicrous. Of course, Fanon did undertake a number of suspicious activities on a daily basis—taking long breaks from the hospital and participating in secret meetings throughout the city—but hardly for the reasons Ben Soltan contended.

Instead, the Minister of Health became increasingly impressed by Fanon, and readily took him up on a proposal to renovate the Hôpital Charles Nicolle into a psychiatric day clinic. This was a relatively new idea, and the clinic would become the first of its kind in all of Africa. Providing psychiatric day services to men-tally ill patients who were otherwise capable of living in the world, the clinic relieved larger hospitals like Manouba from the burden of supporting hundreds of long-term patients night and day, and freed up a large sum of money that could be used for Fanon's proposals. Aside from these economic advantages, Fanon argued that a day clinic was psychologically advantageous to patients as well, as it allowed them to re-integrate with their own social and familial contexts, rather than within the context of an alienating institution. Fanon enlisted the help of his former intern from Blida, Charles Geronomi, who had also come to Tunis.

While the project was a complete success, Fanon was again quick to incur the resentment of his colleagues, who were not as respected or widely published as Fanon, had not won the favor of the Minister of Health, and who viewed his indefatigable energy as sheer exhibitionism. But by now this kind of daily ten-sion was typical for Fanon. He moved his family out of their res-idence at the hospital, taking up residence in a complex owned by the FLN, and he consorted mostly with the interns and nurses who were close to him. Among the hospital staff, only these few persons were able to witness the relaxed side of Fanon. On occasions when the Fanons invited his staff to dinner, Fanon kept them talking about music, food and countless other topics, refilling glasses around the table, until early morning hours. When doctors at last rose to go, Fanon would laugh at their weariness. He once kept the younger Geronomi in drink and conversation until four in the morning. Geronomi entered the hospital the next day to find that Fanon had already been there for some time, and was perplexed by his lateness.

In December of 1958 Fanon asked Geronomi to take charge of the hospital services at the Hôpital Charles Nicolle, offering the brief explanation, "I have to write a book." The explanation was partially true. Fanon would first travel to Accra, the capital of Ghana, as one of five FLN delegates to the first All-Africa People's Conference. He spoke on the violence inherent in colonialism, and remarked that the friendly overtures of decolonization now being made by France to its African colonies were an attempt on the part of France—greatly weakened by the Algerian struggle—to minimize its losses and retain some semblance of post-colonial control in Africa. Fanon was already beginning to set his sights beyond the liberation of Algeria. With colonialism breaking down throughout Africa, an opportunity was emerging to form a new nation from the liberated colonies: a United States of Africa, united and made strong by the reclamation of its land, its resources, and its dignity. This struggle for unity would soon become his primary concern, and he increased his dedication to Algerian liberation, as well as to the emerging revolutionary struggles throughout Africa, on the premise that widespread liberation of African colonies would in the end allow each nation to drop its borders and to unify into a continental world power. In the meantime, he conceived that liberated

African nations could pool their resources, forging an independent African economy and building a legion of African volunteers who could assist toward the liberation of each remaining colony. At Accra he made friends with several other important and like-minded leaders, including Patrice Lumumba, the leader of the nationalist movement in the Belgian Congo, Félix Moumié, confronting French rule in Cameroon, Tom Mboya, leading the struggle for Kenya, and Roberto Holden, who would soon achieve Angola's independence from the Portuguese—all of whom agreed with Fanon as to the imperative value of African unity.

By July Fanon had finished his second book, *L'An Cinq de la Révolution Algérienne* (later published in English as *A Dying Colonialism*). The book includes essays on colonial bias in medicine, the context of the family in Algeria, the misrepresented status of many pro-nationalist Europeans in Algeria, and a highly-controversial essay on the role of women in Islamic culture and in the Algerian revolution in particular. The book went unreviewed in France, even among the radical left, and was soon banned for its pro-Algerian sentiment.

Given his increasing occupation with the FLN and with his plan of a unified Africa, Fanon was little concerned about reviews. By mid-1959 he was almost exclusively preoccupied with "the struggle," and had developed an intense impatience with anything he considered to be inconsequential to that end. Trivial small talk—especially that offered by women—would provoke Fanon to walk off in mid-conversation. If a statement was made that Fanon found untenable, he would first deride the statement, and then the person who had the misfortune of having uttered it. Around Tunis he developed a reputation as being socially harsh, his eyes glaring as he baited people into arguments. The world of Fanon was becoming increasingly divided into those few he could tolerate, and the many he could not.

The FLN assigned him to tour outland refugee camps along the Algerian borders to Tunisia and Morocco in order to improve health conditions and provide impromptu medical services. The sheer magnitude of people in need of basic care was overwhelming, the camps overcrowded with refugees weak and suffering from both the war and the gross lack of nutrition. Fanon could hardly tend to the most pressing maladies at one camp before it was time to move to the next. Then, in midsummer, as Fanon rode in a jeep from one camp to the next along the Algerian-Moroccan border, the jeep struck a mine and sent Fanon soaring, fracturing twelve of his spinal vertebrae. With the lower half of his body paralyzed, he was flown urgently back to Tunis, and then to Rome for more intensive surgery.

In Rome, Fanon met with repeated good fortune. First, the car that was to retrieve him at the airport was demolished when a bomb planted in the engine exploded prematurely on the street. The bomb had all the markings of the *Main Rouge*, a terrorist group of Algerian colonists. His second good fortune lay in the immense skill of his surgeons in Rome, who were able to repair Fanon's spinal damage before paralysis became a permanent condition. The final incident of fortune arose mostly due to Fanon's mounting and ever-justified paranoia when he lay in the hospital attempting to recover, yet noticed with great alarm that the newspaper had printed a small announcement about the arrival of one Doctor Omar—the name under which he had registered at the clinic—which specified not only the clinic but also the number of his room. He immediately called the nurse and insisted that they move him to another room on a different floor, and that they do so as secretly as possible. The staff thought him rather overconcerned about such a tiny matter, but thought again the next morning upon discovering that Fanon's abandoned bed had been machine-gunned to pieces in the middle of the night.

Fanon recuperated, and the bloody war went on. Long before the advisement of his doctors, Fanon returned to work at his clinic and at the Ministry of Information, fervidly debating tactics and revolutionary theory with Malek and Yazid. In Tunis the newly-formed Provisional Government of the Algerian Republic—the GPRA—was beginning to divide between those who supported negotiations with France, and those who believed the struggle should continue until France left Algeria unconditionally. Fanon was uncategorically in the latter camp. He had seen too much Algerian suffering at the hands of the French to allow any concessions. Their most immediate concern was over the predicament of rebel forces in the Algerian interior, now staving off a slow strangulation by French troops on all sides. A plan was conceived to open a new frontier through the Sahara desert along the southern border of Algeria. Such a frontier would open a supply route to the Algerian interior, and could best be maintained with volunteer help from other African nations to the south. As Fanon had consulted with other African leaders on this very subject at the conference in Accra, the GPRA sent him back to Accra for the Second All-African Peoples Conference in January to elicit support for the new southern front.

Arriving at the conference with the highest hopes, Fanon found his optimism difficult to maintain in the days that followed. His own ideas of African unity were fundamentally different from most of the other delegates, who offered measured and conservative speeches about the importance of nationalism and African unity, but seemed little interested in pursuing anything beyond a theoretical conception of the matter. Fanon could not tolerate any diplomacy or theory that was not supported by concrete action. Following a number of tepid speeches, Fanon rose to speak, and immediately seized the atten-

Mohammed Yazid, Minister of
Information for the FLN.
(Algerian National Press and Information
Documentation Center)

Patrice Lumumba, Liberator of the
Congo, 1925–1961.
(AP/Worldwide Photos)

Redha Malek, editor
of *el Moudjahid*.
(Algerian National Press
and Information
Documentation Center)

tion of his audience. As one delegate described it, "I found myself electrified by a contribution that was remarkable not only for its analytical power, but delivered, too, with a passion and brilliance that is all too rare." In the course of his riveting speech, Fanon suddenly stopped, swallowing, as though he were on the verge of losing all composure in a seizure of desperation. When the delegate later introduced himself to Fanon and asked what had happened during the pause, Fanon replied that he was suddenly overwhelmed by his predicament, standing there in front of an assembly of African nationalist leaders, attempting to convince them of the importance of the Algerian struggle at the very moment when men in his country were dying and suffering from torture, and whose cause ought to command the immediate support of "radical and progressive human beings."

Yet his passionate appeal did have an impact on the delegates, and plans for the southern frontier began to materialize. The delegates passed a resolution to begin a new volunteer legion to fight colonialism, beginning in Algeria, and Kwame Nkrumah, the president of Ghana, soon opened two recruitment centers, as did authorities in Egypt. Shortly thereafter, the GPRA appointed Fanon the Algerian Ambassador to Ghana, with the assignment to draw up plans for a southern invasion of Algeria using volunteer forces from the nascent All-African Legion.

Fanon left for Accra again with his family in March. As the representative of Algeria to all of Africa south of the Sahara, Fanon spent several months in almost constant transit, traveling to conferences in Conakry and Addis Ababa, and consulting other African representatives at embassies in Accra. He spent most of the summer in meetings with delegates from Angola, South Africa, Guiana, and Mali, offering lucid and "almost prophetic" analyses of the political predicament in Africa, not only in Algeria but also in Rhodesia, South Africa and the Congo.

Again, his power of speech stirred and inspired those who heard him, and he readily became one of the most influential political figures in Accra, where the whole of Africa converged to discuss its future. Fanon never faltered in relating the struggle in Algeria to his plan for the overthrow of colonialism throughout the continent. He already had plans for a new book, a book that would describe the coming liberation of African nations and outline a theory toward the eventual unification of Africa. His ear pressed to the earth, he could hear the crumbling chains, the "liberating lava" that flowed as the crusts of colonialism began to break apart.

At summer's end negotiations with Mali established the possibility of opening a frontier on the Mali-Algerian border, through a small fertile valley that traversed the southern Sahara. The route still needed to be determined, and intelligence on French forces in the region needed to be gathered. A preliminary scouting trip was planned for late October. Through the fall Fanon was mostly concerned with arrangements for attaining equipment and assembling a volunteer force, and made trips from Accra to Tunis to Rome and back. Having met Félix Moumié of Cameroon en route to Geneva, Fanon arranged to meet him in Rome two weeks later to return to Accra together, and from there travel to the city of Bamako in Mali to begin the Saharan odyssey. In Rome, Moumié never arrived. When Fanon returned to the Accra airport alone, Moumié's father met the lone traveler with a reserved sadness. Their fears were confirmed two days later when they learned the news: Moumié's contact in Geneva had been a French agent, who poisoned his *apéritif* with thallium. After two weeks of sickened agony, Moumié, one of the most vigorous supporters of a unified Africa, was dead. His father absorbed the news with a stoic repetition: "Yes, the program is clear. We must stick to the program."

Fanon left Accra in early November with a short and lean FLN commando, Major Chawki, and they flew west along the rolling African coast toward Conakry in Guinea, their ultimate destination the inland Mali capital of Bamako on the southwestern tip of the Sahara Desert. From there they would cross the open desert toward the Algerian border, burst open the southern front, and transport arms, munitions and Saharan recruits toward Algerian high plateaus. Fanon envisioned the carving out of a wide strait extending deep into the desert to channel the flows of a unified and indomitable force of Malians, Senegalese, Guineans, and Ghanians—climbing the desert slopes and emerging from on high to pour down upon colonial forces with the unmerciful heat of African deliverance.

Already at a stopover in Monrovia, their mission was delayed; in spite of their confirmed reservation on to Conakry, Air France had ironically overbooked, and could not accommodate them until the next day. The airline was particularly obliging, offering to pay any expenses incurred for the inconvenience, and Fanon began to grow suspicious. Wary of anyone of French nationality, Fanon took "the bar-maid allure of a voluble and excruciatingly boring French lady" as the final straw, and the two men skipped out on their flight to enter Guinea by road in the night. The next morning their would-be plane left the ground, turned the opposite direction from its destination, and flew to Abidjan where both passengers and cargo were searched by French soldiers.

From Guinea they crossed into Mali and arrived at Bamako. There a team of eight assembled, adding six sturdy scouts to Chawki and Fanon. On the twenty-second of November the team left early by jeeps toward Timbuktu, trailing the wide Niger River to Ségou, to San, and into green forests at Mopti. On leaving the city a police blockade stopped them for passports. Fanon offered a letter of passage issued by the Minister of

the Interior, but the *gendarmes* demanded their identities. At last
Fanon made himself known to the chief of the post, who prod-
ded for more information until Fanon exploded into an ultima-
tum either to make arrests or to let them pass. A few minutes
later they had moved on, the road disappearing in the thick of
the woods and leaving them to guess their directions. Through
the night they made way blindly to Douentza, then continued at
dawn to clear the forest at Hombori, coming to Gao by late
evening. A Mali commandant prepared them for the trek across
desert terrain. Two days later, in Arab desert gear with guns and
cartridges, they set out toward the Saharan north, forsaking ver-
dant river soils for the red shelter of ridges along the Tilemsi
Valley. Upon reaching Aguerhoc towards midnight they met the
commanders of Mali subdivisions in Kidal and Tessalit. Now
they were ready to discuss terrains and strategies of passage.

Fanon was taken by the thrill of the journey. As they
mounted the desert highlands they could now view the southernmost regions of Algerian desert. Did he want to visit the
frontier at close range? Did he want to see where the French
were building an airport? Under hard red skies they launched
across the frontier and passed a French military camp at Tessalit.
A French solider waved at the passing Arabs in the distance, and
they waved with hearty laughs in return. From here they continued deep into Algeria, enlisting guides, making contact with
nomads, and marking French camps on their maps. The sear of
brightening desert bid them on.

Claude Lanzmann, Jean-Paul Sartre, and Simone de Beauvoir.
(© Bettmann/CORBIS)

10

Into the Sun

> Perhaps Icarus was not as much failing
> as coming to the end of his triumph.
>
> —*Jack Gilbert*

FANON'S RETURN TO ACCRA BROUGHT a notebook filled with sketches and strategic observations, and plans needing little more than approval by the FLN. The Algerian desert was wide open, but the Algerians were not. While they continued to champion Fanon's efforts at establishing a passable supply route to Algerian plateaus from the south, his plans for an All-African Legion had never been a serious consideration for the FLN's primary decision makers. The Algerian rebel army had too many problems dealing with its own interior factions already, and preferred to continue the fight from the established fronts bordering Tunisia and Morocco. Fanon's vision of a great channel through Africa went unrealized.

Fanon also returned to Accra with an overwhelming feeling of exhaustion, a curious condition given the enormous energy he had felt only weeks before. At first surmising that he had overtaxed himself on the Saharan crossing, he allowed himself a short period of rest and recovery. Still the exhaustion remained. A visit to a doctor in Accra informed him that his white blood cell count was abnormally high, and the doctor advised him to consult a hematologist. When he arrived back in Tunis in late December, Josie remarked on the amount of weight he had lost and urged him to visit a doctor again. He simply did not look well, either, and several friends told him as much. At the FLN clinic a fellow doctor studied his blood report with an uncomfortable expression, and after receiving several ambiguous responses to his inquiries, Fanon asked him outright if he had leukemia. He did.

The disease was incurable, and he could not expect to live for more than three or four years. His immediate conclusion was that now he needed to say and do as much as possible in what little time he had left. There was simply so much to do. He had two books in mind to write, and he had committed to assist the revolutionary efforts of Roberto Holden in Angola by overseeing the training of Angolan rebels in FLN training camps. Verging on a state of sheer denial, he continued in this vein for several weeks, training troops and continuing his normally-taxing work schedule. When associates who knew of his illness advised him to spare his energies, he responded with the remark, "Do the colonialists spare us?"

Indeed, they did not. Immediately after learning of the imminence of his own death, Fanon received word of another mortal disappointment: Patrice Lumumba, who had led the liberation of the Congo from Belgium and who resolutely supported the goal of a unified Africa, had been murdered in his own country. As intellectual revolutionaries the two men had grown to respect each other a great deal, and were good friends; Lumumba's death was a stunning blow to Fanon, both for its political and its personal loss. Hope for a unified Africa was being slowly ripped apart at the joints: first Moumié, then Lumumba—and Fanon himself was on limited time.

To further discuss the future of Africa—and more particularly the best direction for the war in Algeria—a conference on anticolonialism brought leading intellectuals to Tunis, including a delegation from Sartre's *Les Temps Modernes*, headed by Claude Lanzmann and Marcel Péju. Knowing Fanon's name from his articles and books, they paid him a visit at home, much to Fanon's ailed enjoyment but to their surprise when they found him sick in bed, his wife vacating the bedroom in tears. They could see at once that Fanon was suffering, but their inquiry about his illness led him promptly to suggest, "Let's talk about something else," and he launched into an analysis of Sartre's recently published *Critique of Dialectical Reason* that went on for hours. His lecture led to a discussion of the Algerian situation, his outrage at the death of Lumumba, and the precarious future of Africa. Lanzmann noted, "He spoke with a voice intensified by urgency; he spoke with the voice of illness. . . . He spoke of his visionary dream of unification for blacks of all countries." Fanon explained how he had sought to train the troops not only physically, but ideologically and morally as well, to prepare them for the stalwart commitment that the struggle for unification would require after Algeria's liberation.

Fanon told Lanzmann and Péju many details about the book he had planned to write on a unified Africa, but which he had now chosen to abandon given the increasing limitations brought on by his health. They urged Fanon to continue the book anyway, perhaps curbing his extensive plans into a shorter, more poignant study. When Fanon assented they made their way from his bedroom to the living room where Josie showed them to the door, offering a thankful but saddened expression.

The quickening deterioration of Fanon's health was disturbing. For over a week he lost his sight and could not even read. After several weeks in bed he felt himself nothing but a dead weight, sinking down into the mattress. In late January he decided to travel to Moscow in search of more specialized treatment. Over the next few weeks, Soviet doctors attempted a number of treatments that were unavailable in North Africa, including a course of Myleran that served to reduce his white blood cell count. Though they offered him every comfort and supplied an informative but disconcerting tour of Soviet psychiatric facilities, their professional advice amounted to the suggestion that his only real hope was to seek treatment in the United States, where new and radical therapies for leukemia were being tested. Fanon at first rejected this idea, as too many African intellectuals had become curiously corrupted after travels to the United States. But on returning to Tunis in mid-February, Fanon made contact with the United States consulate there, who assigned a CIA agent named Oliver Iselin to his case.

By the time Iselin arranged travel, however, Fanon had again changed his mind. In fact he was feeling better than he had felt in a while. With a renewed energy, he set to work on a new book that would combine the most essential elements of his formerly planned study, and that would relate more directly to immediate ideological problems in Algeria. In April he wrote his publisher François Maspero, "The state of my health having improved slightly, I have decided to write something after all. . . . Trusting that you'll satisfy my request, I would like to ask you to speed up the publication of this book: we need it in Algeria and Africa. . . . Ask Sartre to write a preface. . . . "

Another request went to the administration of the Algerian Provisional Government to appoint him as the Algerian ambassador to Cuba. Such an appointment would allow him to return to the Caribbean in his final days, close to his family and familiar surroundings. His request was denied. When his brother Joby came to visit him in Tunis, Frantz spoke about his disappointment on having been denied the post. He told Joby about how their mother had refused his request when he left for the university in France. In some ways he still felt that their mother had not respected his earnest dedication when he left, and he described how he had hoped to return to Martinique in this distinguished position—the young ambassador of a new and great African nation, greeted by the diplomatic corps of the island and worthy of respect by his mother, his old teachers, and anyone who had ever thought him a delinquent rascal who would never amount to anything.

Fanon's final book, *The Wretched of the Earth*, was written in a ten-week blaze of energy in the spring of 1961. Nearly a third of the book was compiled from notes and essays he had already written; among them his speech on colonialism and national culture given at the second Conference of Black Writers and Artists in Rome a few years earlier, and a pointed sample of case history notes and observations from his psychotherapy practices in Blida and Tunis. As promised to Lanzmann and Péju, the study was compressed from a survey of the entire African situation to a piercing and incendiary analysis of colonialism itself—its economic, cultural, and psychological maladies—using examples of the revolution in Algeria as specifics from which to generalize the problem on a worldwide basis. In a sense, by deciding to write less, Fanon said more.

When the book was finished in late spring, Fanon gave the manuscript to Claude Lanzmann, who in turn delivered it to Sartre. In Cuba Sartre found himself in wholehearted agreement with Fanon, and gladly agreed to write the preface. Returning to Rome for the summer, Sartre and de Beauvoir were soon pleased to learn that Fanon was traveling to the north of Italy to treat rheumatism caused by his illness, and wished to visit them in Rome on his way. De Beauvoir and Lanzmann went to meet him at the airport, Lanzmann pointing out a strong but agitated looking man who kept standing up and sitting down again, his gestures abrupt, his eyes darting about in suspicion. Fanon was apparently uneasy about being in Rome again for the first time since the two attempts on his life there, and he began recounting the story of his narrow escapes from death as soon as the two had retrieved him. They drove to meet Sartre for lunch at a café.

Immediately comfortable with Sartre, Fanon showed little anxiety at meeting the philosopher he had so long admired, and leapt at once into open and relaxed discussions of philosophy and politics as though Sartre and de Beauvoir were his longtime friends. One topic led straight to another without pause, and Fanon spoke with restless energy. They remained at the café until two in the morning, when de Beauvoir politely suggested that Sartre needed sleep. Fanon conceded, restraining his usual reprimands for those who fell short of his own endurance, but kept Lanzmann at the table until eight the next morning. "I don't like people who hoard their resources," he pronounced to Lanzmann. Then, laughing, he added, "I'd give twenty thousand francs a day to be able to talk to Sartre from morning to night for two weeks!"

They met again the next day, and spent three days in constant conversation. De Beauvoir admired his spiritedness. "With razor-sharp intelligence, intensely alive, endowed with a grim sense of humor, he explained things, made jokes, questioned us, gave imitations, told stories; everything he talked about seemed to live again before our eyes." But there was also a bleaker side to him: Fanon exaggerated his previous accomplishments in an effort to impress them, though they had made no secret about their admiration of him. He even gave Sartre a curious analysis of his own egotism, asserting that colonization forced one to be vigilantly aware of one's social position, and that one could not allow oneself to forget the need to maintain one's defenses at all times. But did these phenomena really describe the colonized, or did they more describe Fanon? The two philosophers only wondered. Fanon repeatedly disregarded his illness, relating plans as though he had years to live. Yet beneath this surface optimism lingered an incessant preoccupation with disaster, and he assumed the worst possible outcome to every situation with morbid complacency. He briefly admitted that his fierce castigations of the French left's lack of commitment spawned from internal castigations of his own bourgeois intellectual background, and doubts about his own dedication, though still he reproved Sartre for what he viewed as Sartre's failure to commit. They watched him repeatedly reaffirm his commitment to the struggle, as though he still wished to convince himself of it.

On Sunday Fanon caught the train to Abano for rheumatism treatment, and returned ten days later to see the philosophers again before returning to Tunis. He described a chambermaid in Abano who had watched him for several days, and who had finally asked, "Is it true what they say? That you hate white people?" For Fanon the story illustrated one premise: "The heart of the matter is that you white people have a psychological horror of Negroes." When he bid them goodbye, and de Beauvoir shook his feverish hand, she noted, "I seemed to be touching the very passion that was consuming him. He communicated this fire to others; when one was with him, life seemed to be a tragic adventure, often horrible, but of infinite worth."

Though responses from Sartre and others who read the manuscript of *The Wretched of the Earth* were overwhelmingly positive, Fanon expressed the wish that he could have written more, that so much had been left unsaid. But in the early autumn of 1961 he concerned himself more with spending time with his family and enjoying what life could still offer him. He and Josie and their young son relaxed at the beaches of Carthage and spent time with friends in long conversation. Amid peace negotiations occurring between Algeria and France, Fanon still offered his analysis of the Algerian struggle to everyone he spoke with, though it had taken turns quite different from what he once envisioned. There were political reasons for these changes, arising from conflicts for power within the FLN itself; and with similar conflicts dividing the citizens of other emerging African nations, Fanon's vision of a United States of Africa was becoming an increasingly remote possibility. Still he could not dismiss his conviction of the inevitability of African unification, believing its people had only to transgress this phase of "killing each other."

At this point, discussion of these serious topics would soon give way to a slightly affected liveliness in which he set about telling stories and jokes and laughing as much as he could. In fact he laughed a lot, and when others only forced a smile he would laugh all the more, encouraging them to laugh with him. He was a man attempting to enjoy life to the fullest.

He passed through good days and bad days, and in his liveliness he seemed the least willing to admit the truth of his situation. One evening in late September he came to dinner at the house of his friend Doctor Bertène Juminer, whose wife had done her best to cook a West Indian meal for him. Not exhibiting much enthusiasm on eating it, Fanon eventually leaned over to Juminer's wife and suggested, "Next time Michele, no West Indian dinner please."

"We'll make you some couscous next time."

"Good," he replied.

Juminer stole a glance at Josie, who sat reserved despite her suffering, and wondered if they could even expect a next time. Two weeks later Fanon appeared in Juminer's lab with an Algerian colonel and complained of fatigue, instructing Juminer,

"Analyze my blood."

Juminer pierced his finger and watched a drop of blood rise to the surface.

"You don't seem to lack any," he said.

"When can you give me the results?" Fanon asked.

"Tomorrow."

Juminer awaited Fanon's arrival the next day with eager anticipation: the test had proved negative, and Frantz's blood appeared perfectly normal. He conceived that the previous diagnoses had simply been erroneous, and perhaps Fanon's fatigue was due to overwork or parasites.

But Fanon did not share this hope.

"The result does not surprise me," he said. "I am under treatment. It's the Russian medicine, which has diminished the rate of the white globules. My illness nevertheless continues. I'm going to leave for America."

Fanon made contact with the American agent Oliver Iselin again, and was soon on his way to the United States with the aid of the Algerian Mission to Washington and the United States Department of State. During a stopover in Rome, Sartre came by to visit him, but Fanon was in a terrible condition. He lay flat on his bed, unable to speak, his face tense. His only act of revolt against the illness that seized him was a constant shifting from one position to another. After several hours of sitting with Fanon, the saddened philosopher left.

Fanon arrived in the United States on the first Tuesday in October, and was checked into the Dupont Plaza Hotel in Washington. Despite his worsening condition, Fanon was not admitted to the National Institute of Health until the following Tuesday, and mysteriously remained in the Plaza Hotel for a week, with only a personal nurse and the daily visits of Oliver Iselin for company. Finally he was admitted to the Clinical Center in Bethesda, Maryland, where he registered as Ibrahim Fanon—a rather thin disguise—and, after the suspiciously prolonged delay, refused to provide specific answers to their medical questions. His doctor, however, a gentle young hematologist named David Heywood, at once put him at ease. Though Heywood showed limited political interest, the two men spent long periods in discussion of medicine and psychiatry and attendant social issues, and Heywood was happy to keep Fanon informed about every small detail of his illness and treatment.

His second regular associate became agent Oliver Iselin, who visited him on a daily basis—partially on assignment, and partially because he was developing an immense admiration of Fanon during their brief association. His attempts at soliciting information were largely futile, Fanon answering his questions with long diatribes on colonialism, Western imperialism, and the state of the Third World. In the course of discussions the two men developed an adversarial friendship, and on his better days nurses noted that Fanon seemed eagerly to await the arrival of Iselin, and to anticipate their spirited conversations.

Fanon suffered several cataclysmic hemorrhages, the rising leukocytic fire that coursed through his veins bursting forth in an eruption that pushed him to the verge of total collapse. Nurses attended him day and night, injecting him with vital plasma. They attempted several complete transfusions, hoping to shock his immune system into a coordinated response. All to little avail. After several weeks of intense treatment, it became apparent that there would be no quick recovery, and Fanon would not be returning to North Africa.

In early November Iselin brought Josie and young Olivier to Washington from Tunis, and Frantz wrote Joby to inform him that his chronic leukemia had now become acute leukemia, but that things were "a little better" with the arrival of his wife and son. Young Olivier, on beholding his father connected to tubes and bags, fled the room to alert his mother that the bad men had cut his daddy up with knives. Indeed, this seemed not far from the truth, and amid the mounting hopelessness Fanon himself began to resume his former distrust of the hospital staff, and of all Americans, for that matter. He spent his more able hours writing letters to his mother, his family, and persons he deemed worthy of the immense effort writing required. A brief period of remission allowed him to appreciate newly-printed copies of *The Wretched of the Earth*, and to speak weakly of future studies, perhaps on the psychological effects of death itself. He received visits from Alioune Diop, Roberto Holden, and Claude Lanzmann, who flew to Washington just to see him. In Paris his new book had been released to the highest public praise, and his name was on every lip, his face on the cover of every liberal magazine. In spite of these victories he knew he fought a losing battle, and his only response to the news of his success was, "That's not going to get me my marrow back."

To one friend he wrote of the frustration he suffered at facing such a defeat:

> What I want to say is that death is always close by, and what's important is not to know if you can avoid it, but to know that you have done the most possible to realize your ideas. . . . We are nothing on earth if we are not, first of all, slaves of a cause, the cause of the people, the cause of justice, the cause of liberty.

Yet here he was made to lay supine, enduring futile efforts to maintain his insurgent blood, with the repetition of transfusions seeming evermore ineffectual and pointless. On the morning of the first Wednesday in December, Frantz greeted Josie with the dejected remark, "Last night they put me in the washing machine again." She ran her fingertips along the lines of his face, felt the cool dew that layered the swelter within. Some while later his breath gave out. Fanon lay struggling and conscious while doctors and nurses fought to save him, but they could not.

The Algerian government, still fighting in the course of peace negotiations with the French, sent a special airplane to Washington with an envoy to bring the body of Frantz Fanon back to Tunis. His wife and son also returned, accompanied by a respectful Oliver Iselin. In Tunis the coffin containing Fanon's body, draped by the Algerian flag, was placed in the airport's *Salon d'Honneur,* where militants and leaders from the FLN and from numerous African nations paid their final respects, showering wreaths and flowers upon the coffin. Fanon had requested a burial in Algeria, and on the twelfth day of December twenty official cars, amid saluting guerillas and solemn adornments of national ceremony, followed his lifeless body from the city and into the mountain region that separates Tunisia from Algeria. By foot a detachment of Algerian soldiers carried the casket on branches deep into the thick woods, resting it on a bed of lentisk and cork. In the distance the wrath of artillery thundered, and two jets passed overhead as the war went on around them. Over the grave as Fanon was interred, a commandant pledged their commitment to the day that the resting place of Fanon could be moved from this forest outland to the deepest heart of Algeria, and they bid their companion farewell.

Three months after Fanon's burial—the first national funeral of the Algerian nation—freedom for Algeria was attained through a settlement with France on the nineteenth day of March, 1962. Terrorist acts by Europeans remaining in Algeria continued through the spring, and General Raoul Salan—unaccepting of his second defeat since Indo-China—was arrested in April on the charge of terrorism. In May, as hundreds of Europeans left Algeria each day, a "scorched earth" policy among evacuating French militants saw to the destruction of hundreds of schools and public buildings with the sentiment that Muslim Algerians should not have them. Yet the Algerians gradually rebuilt their nation—though among heavy internal strife and conflicts between factions, with many of their own heroes assassinated or forced into exile.

As Fanon had feared might occur, the elite layer of Europeans in Algeria was promptly supplanted by an elite layer of bourgeois Algerians who sought little more than to snatch appropriated European privileges into their own hands. In this sense, colonialism went undefeated. Widespread poverty and social inequity persisted, and manipulation of power ensured that the FLN remained an unchallenged political party in democratic Algeria in the following decades. Throughout the rest of Africa, similar tales played out: internal conflicts arose, mostly from economic and political strangleholds exacted upon these small nations by their former or continuing colonizers. With no central voice to provide a compelling rhetoric and to maintain focus on the aim of unity, Africa remained fractured. In Mali, in Ghana, in Nigeria, in Sierra Leone and in the Congo, military coups seized power. South Africa soon began a long and lonesome fight against Afrikaner minority rule under the leadership of Nelson Mandela, and throughout the continent the bitter ravages of subjugation and discrimination continued to disrupt the freedom of every African consciousness. The Caribbean colonies remained more benign in their conflict, and while many islands retained a small political movement toward nationalization, the explosion of tourism in the latter half of the twentieth century diminished popular support toward this end. Still the majority of land and commerce is under control of small

The Empress Josephine, décapité, defaced with red paint, on the Savane in Fort-de-France.
(Photo by author)

handfuls of the population.

In Martinique the name of Fanon remained unknown for some time. For many years he was considered a traitor. Fanon's daughter Mireille, who did not see her father after her earliest days, traveled to Martinique with her uncle Joby as a young graduate and became better acquainted with her family there. In 1984, Marcel Manville founded the *Cercle Frantz Fanon*, a political action group dedicated to carrying on the ideals of his boyhood friend. Not long after, Aimé Césaire, who would be elected as mayor of Fort-de-France for forty-five years in a row, changed the name of a major avenue in the city to Avenue Frantz Fanon, and supervised the construction of a small outdoor theater on the *Savane* titled the Forum Frantz Fanon, intended as a forum for public discussion and exchange of ideas in the spirit of his former pupil and friend. Yet Joby protests, "They discuss the name of Fanon, but they do not discuss his *ideas*."

In Algiers as well one can walk along a major boulevard that bears the title of Frantz Fanon, and a literary prize in his name was instituted under the presidency of Ahmed Ben Bella. Nurses at Blida-Joinville petitioned to change the name of the hospital to the Frantz Fanon Psychiatric Institute, but the greater legacy there lies in the ongoing continuation of the changes he instituted. Algeria's most prestigious psychiatric hospital still boasts a beautiful and prolific garden, tended to entirely by patients.

Fanon's ideas are possibly discussed nowhere more than in the country of his death, where repeated rekindlings of interest have kept his thought aflame. His second arrival on the shores of America came with translations of all his works into English in 1966 and 1967, and he was ushered at once to the discussion halls among members of the American Black Liberation Movement. Fanon's powerful voice spoke plainly and forcefully in accompaniment to the cry for social justice that crossed the nation, and Eldridge

Cleaver dubbed the publication of an English version of *The Wretched of the Earth* as "itself an historical event" that would later become "known among militants of the Black Liberation Movement in America as 'The Bible.'" Fanon was carried and studied by James Forman, LeRoi Jones, and Howard Fuller, among countless others, and his thought readily influenced Stokely Carmichael and the foundation of the Black Power Movement.

After much controversy on Fanon owing mostly to an overemphasis on his theory of the function of violence, attention to Fanon subsided along with much of the Black Power dialogue, only to reemerge gradually on university campuses for discussion by a far wider audience. In seminars and conferences his name again flourished, now giving greater emphasis to the core of his contributions, to his humanism, and to his piercing psychological insights. The overarching breadth of his interests has assured that his theories are equally relevant to studies of psychology, of political science, of literature, of culture, of race relations, of sociology, and of philosophy. Interpretations in each camp continue to proliferate, as do names and labels employed to describe him. Yet for all descriptions, we will always lack one: a description of that essence of self that names ineluctably fail to make clear, be it even a name so distinguished as the name Frantz Fanon.

ACKNOWLEDGEMENTS

My deepest gratefulness is due to Joby Fanon and France-Line Fanon, who took time from their busy schedules to consult with me and aided in my search for Fanon materials. Also thanks to Charles Noëlé, of the Departmental Archives in Martinique, who drove me to the university in Schoelcher and showed me around campus without even knowing my name. My publisher and editor, respectively Gwendolin Herder and Barbara Ellis, deserve considerable appreciation for their assistance and faith in this project. I also am grateful to Jeremy Sharpe for his political consultations, to my parents for their unwavering support, and to Kimberly, for much of the above, and much more.

CHRONOLOGY

1925   Born in Fort-de-France, Martinique, on July 20.

1939   Fanon begins attending lycée Schoelcher in Fort-de-France; studies French under Aimé Césaire during his last year 1940.

1943   Leaves for Dominica to join the Free French Forces; returns shortly thereafter.

1944   In April Fanon leaves for France to fight against the Nazis. After a brief stay in North Africa, he participates in Operation Dragoon when Allied forces invade southern France. In late November he is seriously wounded, and removed from the fighting for three months.

1945   Fanon is awarded the Croix de Guerre by Colonel Salan for outstanding courage in action; returns home to Martinique in October.

1946   Fanon completes baccalaureate degree at lycée Schoelcher, then works for Césaire's election campaign in the summer before leaving for Paris. After a few weeks in Paris, he moves to Lyon to enroll in medical school.

1947   Attends University of Lyon.

1951   Defends dissertation, earns doctorate in psychiatry.

1952   Publishes first book, *Peau Noire, Masques Blancs*; marries Marie-Josephe Dublé from Lyon.

1953   Passes *Médicat*, becomes *chef de service* at Blida-Joinville in Algeria.

1925   Malcom X, Félix Moumié and Patrice Lumumba born.

1939   Young Aimé Césaire returns to Martinique, begins
        teaching at lycée Schoelcher and publishes his first
        long poem, *Cahier d'un Retour au Pays Natal.*

1940   The Germans invade France on May 10. Vichy gov-
        ernment installed. Admiral Robert lands his fleet on
        Martinique.

1943   Admiral Robert challenged by Colonel Tourtet; leaves
        Martinique with his fleet in early summer.

1945   May 8: "V.E.-Day," Axis powers surrender. On the
        same day, massacre at Setif, Algeria.

1946   Césaire wins election; Martinique changed from a
        French colony to an overseas department.

1947   India is proclaimed independent and partitioned into
        India and Pakistan.

1952   Peace treaty with Japan signed in San Francisco.
        Julius and Ethel Rosenberg are sentenced to death for
        espionage against the U.S.

1953   Vietnamese rebels attack Laos.
        Queen Elizabeth II crowned.

1956   Joins Algerian liberation effort. Addresses the First Congress of Black Writers and Artists in Paris. Resigns his post at Blida-Joinville.

1957   Expelled from Algeria. Travels briefly to Paris and then to Tunis to join the Front for National Liberation (FLN). Works on editorial staff of *el Moudjahid*.

1958   Participates as a member of the Algerian delegation in the first All-African People's Conference in Accra, Ghana.

1959   Addresses the Second Congress of Black Writers and Artists in Rome. Is hospitalized in Rome after his jeep strikes a landmine; narrowly escapes assassination. Publishes *L'An Cinq de la Révolution Algérienne*.

1960   Participates in the Second All-African People's Conference in Accra, becomes permanent Ambassador to Ghana for the Provisional Algerian Government.

1961   Learns he has Leukemia, publishes *Les Damnés de la Terre*. Dies on December 6 in Washington, D.C. Returned to Tunisia to be buried in Algerian territory.

1964   *Pour la Révolution Africaine* published posthumously.

1954   Revolutionary war breaks out in Algeria on November 1.
U.S. Supreme Court rules that segregation by color in
public schools is a violation of the 14th Amendment to
the U.S. Constitution.

1956   Tunisia and Morocco win independence from the French.
Pakistan becomes Islamic republic.
Jordan and Israel accept UN truce proposals.

1957   International Atomic Energy Agency established.
Albert Camus wins Nobel Prize for Literature.

1958   Guinea wins its independence.
West Indies Federation is in force.
Egypt and Syria join to form the United Arab
Republic.
European Common Market comes into being.

1959   Fidel Castro becomes Premier of Cuba.

1960   Mali, Niger, Chad, Senegal, Mauritania, the Congo,
Cameroon and Gabon win independence or are
granted independent status in attempts to curb revolutionary action.

1961   Cuban exiled rebels attempt an unsuccessful invasion
of Cuba at the Bay of Pigs.
"Freedom Riders," white and black liberals loosely
organized to test and force integration in the South,
are attacked and beaten by white citizens.

1962   March 19: Algeria wins its independence.
U.S. military council established in S. Vietnam.

1964   Martin Luther King, Jr. publishes "Why We Can't Wait."

NOTES

CHAPTER 2: MORNE NOIRE

The account of St. Pierre and the eruption of Mt. Pelée abbreviates a far more extended description made by Michel Tauriac in *La Catastrophe* (1982), the first book of his trilogy *Années Créoles*, especially pp. 402–424. Descriptions of the more prolonged drama of Martinican society in the early twentieth century, its racial and social relations, and the centrality of language to the French project of assimilation are central to Fanon's *Black Skin, White Masks*, and are also discussed in his essay, "West Indians and Africans" from *Toward the African Revolution*, particularly pp. 19–24.

Other than his own published accounts in the above two sources, any accounts of Fanon's early family life are derived from Joby Fanon, either from stories he relayed to the author in Martinique on March 20, 2000, or from the article "Pour Frantz, Pour Notre Mère" published in *Sans Frontière*, pp. 5–11. The two accounts tended to overlap. Any quoted material is taken directly from the *Sans Frontière* article, and translated by the author. Some further genealogical information was supplied and confirmed by France-Line Fanon. Finally, the tale of Madame Fanon posting a sign to retrieve her husband and of Frantz's composure in the pistol accident owe credit to Hussein Abdilahi Bulhan, who heard both stories from Félix Fanon in 1982, and both are published in *Frantz Fanon and the Psychology of Oppression*, pp. 19 and 20, respectively.

Chapter 3: War from Within, War from Without

Descriptions of Martinique between 1939 and 1943, the influential arrival of Césaire, and the impact of Vichy occupation of the island on its inhabitants again comes from Fanon's "West Indians and Africans" on pp. 19–24. Similar accounts of this period can be found in Marcel Manville's memoir *Les Antilles Sans Fard*, pp. 23–36, reiterating much of what he states in earlier articles about his childhood with Fanon, particularly "Témoignage d'un Ami et d'un Compagnon de Lutte" found in *L'Actualité de Frantz Fanon*, pp. 11–23, and in "Hommage à Frantz Fanon," found in *Sans Frontière*, pp. 35–37. This latter article also describes Fanon's intervention with the young pickpocket beaten by French sailors on p. 15, and refers to Fanon's theft from his mother's shop before leaving for Dominique on p. 16.

Accounts of the *Bande Raide* and Fanon's childhood shenanigans, of the Fanon boys' stay with Uncle Edouard, and of their parents' argument over this matter come from Joby Fanon's "Pour Frantz." The speech made by M. Joseph-Henri comes from this article as well, and was recited to the author verbatim and without preparation by Joby Fanon on March 20, 2000. Both the article and the interview also provide details on Félix's wedding day and Frantz Fanon's departure for Dominica, including the theft of his father's fabric to pay the ferryman. It should be noted that Josie Fanon wrote a letter to Irene Gendzier, which asserted that Fanon went to St. Lucia to join the Free French Forces, and not Dominica. When asked about this possibility, Joby Fanon stated that it was out of the question. Since he was present at the time and Josie Fanon was not, one tends to credit the latter, and geography also supports his version. Geismar, Zahar and Pirelli all make reference to Fanon leaving for Dominica with two friends, and according to Geismar, one of them was Manville. However, Manville makes no mention of this in his memoir or elsewhere despite his many descriptions of Fanon's flight to Dominica, and his vivid description of events in Martinique during Fanon's absence indicates that he was in Martinique at the time.

Zahar's biographical information on Fanon derives solely from Pirelli, and Pirelli does not offer sources, though this fact may have come from Geismar. Joby Fanon maintains that Fanon was alone when he left. General relations within the family come from "Pour Frantz," and from descriptions provided by France-Line Fanon. Other details of Fanon's adolescence in Martinique are scattered through *Black Skin, White Masks*. Finally, some further information about Césaire and about Martinique at this period was gleaned from an article in a recent *Monthly Review*, "A Poetics of Anticolonialism" by D.G. Kelley, pp. 4–7, and from the film *Aimé Césaire: Une Voix pour l'Histoire*, directed by Euzhan Palcy.

Chapter 4: Motherland

Accounts of events leading up to the fall of Admiral Robert are available in Marcel Manville's *Antilles*, pp. 27–36. Some details also come from Geismar, *Fanon*, 26–28. Details about Frantz's return to Martinique and his studies and activities in this period mostly come from Joby Fanon's "Pour Frantz," and from his discussions with the author. His repeated attempts to persuade Frantz not to join the war effort were emphasized in this interview. The day of departure is recounted by J. Fanon, Ibid., p. 7, and Manville, Ibid., pp. 45–46.

Most information about Frantz's activities in the war ultimately traces to Manville. Details of their departure, crossing the Atlantic, life at Guercif, the "whitening" of the French division, and various battles including Fanon's major injury come from "Témoignage," pp. 17–18, "Hommage," pp. 36–37, and *Antilles*, pp. 37–46. Some further details, in particular their interrogation by the four French officers, his practical joke with the film, the death of Fanon's sentry replacement, and Fanon's first minor injury come from Geismar, *Fanon*, pp. 31–40 (and these presumably come from Geismar's interviews with Manville).

All correspondence is translated by the author from Joby Fanon's article "Pour Frantz." A few details on the war issue from Fanon himself, such as his surprise at the animosity of Algerian locals, the French military attitude toward the Senegalese, and the sending of Senegalese to fight a machine-gun nest, are all described in *Black Skin, White Masks*. Details of the invasion of southern France, the specific dates of battles, and the movements of French troops throughout the war are taken from Winston Churchill's *Triumph and Tragedy*, most especially on pp. 96–99, 264–266, and pp. 414–417. Churchill provides numerous maps and facts that were invaluable in reconstructing events and substantiating Manville's recollections nearly fifty years later. Considering that Churchill's accounts of the war had every cause for bias, a few confirming details were sought in Martin Gilbert's *The Second World War*.

CHAPTER 5: RETURN HOME

Fanon's letter of April 12 has been widely published in French literature on Fanon since its discovery in 1981. The letter is invariably taken at face value and its context is never questioned, though there are some ambiguities surrounding this letter that remain unaddressed. Though it is often presumed the letter was written on the battlefield, as the letter clearly implies, the date of the letter places its origination at a time *after* the West Indian soldiers were removed from battle and returned to Toulon: March 30, 1945. This date is given by Manville, and his recollection of this event as simultaneous with the crossing of the Rhine by the French division perfectly matches published historical accounts.

However, most references to Fanon's letter seem to ignore the fact that it was dated in early April, including Manville's own citation of it in *Antilles* (pp. 241–242) where he states the letter was written during fighting at the *Poche de Colmar*, which was completely cleared of German forces by February 9 by all historical accounts.

This author would incline to presume that some error was made about the date the letter was written, were it not for Fanon's statement of the date in the very first sentence, which is clearly discernable in Fanon's handwriting in a facsimile of the letter printed in *Sans Frontière* on p. 37. A few possibilities remain: (1) that Fanon wrote the letter during battle as stated by Manville, but wrote the wrong date or recopied it in April before sending it; (2) that Fanon was assigned to an unknown "perilous mission" after the West Indian soldiers left northern France and were resting in Toulon (fighting also continued in nearby Italy at this time); or (3) that the letter was not written before a "perilous mission," but that this claim was made for literary effect because it best reflected Fanon's sentiments about the war that he wished to express, however belated in actuality. The facts in this matter will likely remain unknown. All details of the soldiers' mistreatment in Toulon after the German surrender come from Manville's *Antilles*, pp. 47–48, and from Fanon himself in *Black Skin, White Masks*, p. 156.

The account of the chateau at Bois-Guillaume, of the dinner with the French family, and of the return to Martinique, come from Manville, *Antilles*, pp. 49–54. Fanon's general malaise was described by Joby to Irene Gendzier and is found in her *Frantz Fanon*, p. 15, and is also alluded to in his "Pour Frantz" article. Césaire's political campaign is detailed in Palcy's film *Aimé Césaire*, and the involvement of Joby and Frantz is described in Geismar's *Fanon*, pp. 40–42. Césaire's speech is cited from the memory of Frantz Fanon and printed in *Black Skin, White Masks*.

Also in Geismar are some details of Fanon's departure for Paris on pp. 43–44, likewise recounted by Manville, *Antilles*, p. 242. Geismar dates Fanon's arrival in France as late January, 1947, after the death of his father, the error of which is manifest by Fanon's letter from Lyon to his mother on learning the news of his father's death. Other accounts, such as Pirelli, *Fanon*, p. 122, offer the more likely arrival date of 1946.

Many details of Fanon's life as a student come from Geismar, *Fanon*, pp. 46–49, who interviewed some of Fanon's classmates and professors, and Gendzier, *Fanon*, pp. 16–17, as well as a bit from Simone de Beauvoir's *La Force des Choses*, though the greatest source of his interior life at this period is found in *Black Skin, White Masks*, particularly chapters 1, 5 and 6, the character of which is unapproachable in attempts at summation. Information about his father's death comes from J. Fanon's "Pour Frantz" article, as do the two letters cited here. Details regarding events leading to Fanon's first child were reported in Geismar, *Fanon*, p. 47. His relationship with Josie is described in Geismar, *Fanon*, p. 52, and Gendzier, *Fanon*, p. 17.

Some analysis and observations regarding Fanon's medical thesis are indebted to a fascinating study made by B. Marie Perinbam in *Holy Violence*, pp. 21–25. Lévy-Bruhl's theories are best described in his *The 'Soul' of the Primitive* and in *How Natives Think*, of which the author's comprehension owes heavily to the explanations of Serge Moscovici. Further details on Fanon's thesis and late academic career were described in an interview with Joby Fanon. The article he published in *Esprit*, "The 'North African Syndrome,'" is reprinted in *Toward the African Revolution*. Fanon's interactions with Francis Jeanson are described in the preface and the lengthy postface Jeanson wrote in the second French edition of *Peau Noire, Masques Blancs*. The dedication to Félix on Fanon's thesis comes from Geismar, *Fanon*, p. 11, and most information on this 1952 interval in Martinique comes from Geismar's *Fanon*, pp. 13, 16, 21–22.

Chapter 7: Liberator of Minds

Geismar offers a fair summary of Fanon's internship with Tosquelles on pp. 53–56, but a far more comprehensive account is available in Gendzier, *Fanon*, pp. 63–71. It also should be noted that Geismar's chronology sometimes fails to add up, and though he infers (if one applies some arithmetic to his claims) that Fanon began his residency at Saint-Alban in 1951, this appears unlikely when considering the date of his thesis defense and Joby Fanon's account of their extended return to Martinique in February of 1952. Pirelli, *Fanon*, p. 123, also places Fanon at Saint-Alban beginning in mid-1952. The sensible conclusion is that Fanon spent only one year at Saint-Alban, and not two as Geismar asserts. If there is another sensible conclusion, this author cannot think what it would be.

Fanon's interest in Trotsky is noted by Gendzier, *Fanon*, p. 20. Fanon's interest in Richard Wright is evinced by the letter he wrote to Wright from Saint-Alban on January 6, 1953, and was further explicated by Joby Fanon when questioned by the author. Both of these items contradict the prevalent belief that Fanon always despised the United States and viewed it as a lost cause in the struggle for racial equality. Rather, it seems Fanon held a great deal of hope for the United States as one country that promised any possibility of racial integration and transcendence of its history of oppression. That he was mistrustful of the American tradition of corporate imperialism is without dispute; it seems his attitude, at least in 1953, was one of ambiguous but optimistic hopefulness.

Details of Fanon's participation in the Médicat are described in Geismar, *Fanon*, p. 57–58, and are recounted with some minor differences by Joby Fanon in the film directed by Isaac Julien, *Black Skin, White Mask*. Where the two differed, preference is here given to Joby Fanon's account. Julien's film is also the source of Frantz's remarks to Joby about his dissatisfaction at Pontorson. The story of Director Kriff's reaction to the soccer game was relayed by France-Line Fanon. An overview of Fanon's life at Blida-Joinville comes from Geismar, *Fanon*, pp. 62–68 and pp. 84–88, though a more thorough and critical account of Fanon's work and theoretical development there can be found in Gendzier, *Fanon*, pp. 72–88. Some description of Fanon's interactions with interns and nurses comes from Alice Cherki, "Témoignage d'une Militante Algérienne," in *Mémorial*

International Frantz Fanon collected by the Comité Frantz Fanon, pp. 181–185.

CHAPTER 8: REVOLUTION

Fanon's letter to his family on the death of his sister Gabrielle comes from Joby Fanon in "Pour Frantz," p. 11, and is translated by the author. Accounts of Manville's visits to the Fanons in Blida come mostly from Manville's *Antilles*, pp. 149–158, and pp. 243–244. The story of Fanon's charge on the police checkpoint comes from Geismar, *Fanon*, p. 70. The Massacre at Cazouna is relayed by Manville in *Antilles*, pp. 156–158, and a similar event is described in Geismar, *Fanon*, with rather different details. The version here is entirely from Manville.

Details about Pierre Chaulet come from Horne, *A Savage War of Peace*, p. 139, and Geismar, p. 93–94. Details about Salan and Lacoste come from Horne, *Savage*, p. 154 and p. 179 respectively. Information about Dr. Lacaton's arrest and some of Fanon's military activities come from Geismar, *Fanon*, pp. 76–78. Clinical accounts come from Fanon's *The Wretched of the Earth*, and Fanon's resignation letter can be found in its entirety as "Letter to the Resident Minister (1956)" in *Toward the African Revolution*, pp. 52–54. Jeanson's observations come from his postface to *Peau Noire*. The conversation between Joby and Frantz regarding Frantz's departure for Tunisia was described to the author in an interview with Joby Fanon, and further information about Fanon's brief stay in France comes from Manville's *Antilles*, pp. 239–150, and from an interview with Joby Fanon.

CHAPTER 9: THE STRUGGLE

Details of Fanon's work and interactions at Manouba come from Geismar, *Fanon*, pp. 128–140. Geismar also provides some details about the First All-African Peoples Conference on pp. 159–162, as does Peter Worsley, the delegate in the audience, who describes the conference in "Frantz Fanon: Revolutionary Theories" in *The Monthly Review* (May, 1969), pp. 30–31.

Fanon's injury on the Moroccan-Algerian border and subsequent events in Italy are relayed by Bertène Juminer's contribution to "Hommages à Frantz Fanon" from *Présence Africaine* (Second Trimester, 1962), p. 126, and similarly by Simone de Beauvoir in *La Force des Choses*, p. 619.

Fanon's influence among ambassadors in Accra in the summer of 1960 is attested to by H.E. Mahmoud Mestiri in his brief testimonial, "Frantz Fanon: A Spokesman for the Third World," in the United Nations publication *International Tribute to Frantz Fanon*, p. 9. The accounts of Fanon's trek across the Sahara come from Fanon's notes printed in *Toward the African Revolution*, pp. 177–189. Note that the introduction to the notes claims the trek occurred during the summer of 1960, though the notes themselves clearly begin in the autumn of that year, and indicate that the trek commenced in late November.

CHAPTER 10: INTO THE SUN

Fanon's initial contact with Lanzmann and Péju in Tunis is described by Lanzmann in Annie Cohen-Solal's *Sartre*, p. 431, and in de Beauvoir's memoir *La Force des Choses*, p. 609. Fanon's letter to Maspero of April 7, 1961, comes from the Maspero archives and is cited in Cohen-Solal's *Sartre*, p. 433. Frantz's disappointment on refusal of the post as Ambassador to Cuba comes from Gendzier, *Fanon*, p. 16. Sartre and de Beauvoir's interactions with Fanon are related in de Beauvoir's *Force des Choses*, pp. 619–624, and this is also the source of some information on Fanon's hospital stay and eventual death, along with Geismar, *Fanon*, pp. 182–187, and Gendzier, *Fanon*, pp. 231–233. The letter cited can be found in Geismar, *Fanon*, p. 185. Details of Fanon's funeral come from "Les damnés de la terre" in *el Moudjahid*, (December 21, 1961).

BIBLIOGRAPHY

BOOKS BY FANON

Peau Noire, Masques Blancs, Paris: Éditions du Seuil, 1952. *Black Skin, White Masks*, trans. Charles Lam Markmann, New York: Grove Press, 1967.

L'An Cinq de la Révolution Algérienne, Paris: Maspero, 1959. *A Dying Colonialism*, trans. Haakon Chevalier, New York: Grove Press, 1965.

Les Damnés de la Terre, Paris: Maspero, 1961. *The Wretched of the Earth*, trans. Constance Farrington, New York: Grove Press, 1968.

Pour la Révolution Africaine, Paris: Maspero, 1964. *Toward the African Revolution*, trans. Haakon Chevalier, New York: Grove Press, 1969.

BOOKS ABOUT FANON

Aruffo, Alessandro & Pirelli, Giovanni. *Frantz Fanon: o l'Eversione Anticoloniale*, Rome: Erre Emme Edizioni, 1994.

Bouvier, Pierre. *Fanon*, Paris: Éditions Universitaires, 1971.

Bulhan, Hussein Abdilahi. *Frantz Fanon and the Psychology of Oppression*, New York: Plenum Press, 1985.

Caute, David. *Frantz Fanon*, New York: The Viking Press, 1970.

Cohen-Solal, Annie. *Sartre 1905–1980*, Paris: Gallimard, 1985. Trans. Anna Cancogni, *Sartre: A Life*, New York: Random House, 1987.

Comité Frantz Fanon. *Mémorial International Frantz Fanon*, Paris: Présence Africaine, 1984.

Dacy, Elo. *L'Actualité de Frantz Fanon: Actes du Colloque de Brazzaville (12–16 Décembre 1984)*, Paris: Éditions Karthala, 1986.

De Beauvoir, Simone. *La Force des Choses*, Paris: Gallimard, 1963.

Fontenot, Chester J. *Frantz Fanon: Language as the God Gone Astray in the Flesh*, Lincoln, Nebr.: University of Nebraska Press, 1979.

Geismar, Peter. *Fanon*, New York: Dial Press, 1971.

Gendzier, Irene L. *Frantz Fanon: A Critical Study*, New York: Grove

Press, 1973.

Gordon, Lewis R. *Fanon and the Crisis of European Man: An Essay on Philosophy and the Human Sciences*, New York: Routledge, 1995.

Gordon, Lewis, Sharpley-Whiting, T. Denean, & White, Renée T. (eds.). *Fanon: A Critical Reader*, Oxford: Blackwell Publishers, 1996.

Hansen, Emmanuel. *Frantz Fanon: Social and Political Thought*, Ohio State University Press, 1977.

Horne, Alistair. *A Savage War of Peace: Algeria 1954–1962*, New York: The Viking Press, 1977.

Makward, Christiane P. *Mayotte Capécia ou l'Aliénation Selon Fanon*, Paris: Éditions Karthala, 1999.

Manville, Marcel. *Les Antilles sans Fard*, Paris: L'Harmattan, 1992.

McCulloch, Jock. *Black Soul, White Artifact: Fanon's Clinical Psychology and Social Theory*, Cambridge: Cambridge University Press, 1983.

Onwuanibe, Richard C. *A Critique of Revolutionary Humanism: Frantz Fanon*, St. Louis: Warren H. Green, 1983.

Perinbam, Marie B. *Holy Violence: The Revolutionary Thought of Frantz Fanon*, Washington, D.C.: Three Continents Press, 1982.

Pirelli, Giovanni. *Fanon*, Rome: Erre Emme Edizioni, 1971.

Sekyi-Otu, Ato. *Fanon's Dialectic of Experience*, Cambridge, Massachusetts: Harvard University Press, 1996.

Sharpley-Whiting, T. Denean. *Frantz Fanon: Conflicts and Feminisms*, Lanham, Maryland: Rowman & Littlefield Publishers, 1998.

Wyrick, Deborah. *Fanon for Beginners*, New York: Writers and Readers, 1998.

Zahar, Renate. *Kolonialismus und Entfremdung*, Frankfurt am Main: Verlagsanstalt, 1969. Trans. Roger Dangeville, *L'Oeuvre de Frantz Fanon: Colonialisme et Aliénation dans l'Oeuvre de Frantz Fanon*, Paris: Maspero, 1970.

ARTICLES

Berque, Jacques; Césaire, Aimé; Chanderli, A.; Domenach, Jean-Marie; Juminer, Bertène; Lacouture, Jean; Maspero, François; Morin, Edgar; Nkrumah, Kwame; Stibbd, Pierre, "Hommages à Frantz Fanon." *Présence Africaine* (1962): 118–141.

Fanon, Joby, "Pour Frantz, Pour Notre Mère." *Sans Frontière* (Feb. 1982): 5–11.

Geismar, Peter, "A Biographical Sketch." *Monthly Review* 21 (May

1969): 22–30.

Hansen, Emmanuel, "Frantz Fanon: Portrait of a Revolutionary Intellectual." *Transition* 46 (1974): 25–46.

Manville, Marcel, "Hommage à Frantz Fanon," *Sans Frontière* (Feb. 1982): 35–37.

Worsley, Peter, "Revolutionary Theories." *Monthly Review* 21 (May 1969): 30–49.

FILMS

Julien, Isaac (dir), *Black Skin, White Mask*, San Francisco: California Newsreel, 1996.

Palcy, Euzhan (dir), *Aimé Césaire: Une Voix pour l'Histoire*, San Francisco: California Newsreel, 1994.

OTHER SOURCES

Césaire, Aimé. *Cahier d'un Retour au Pays Natal*, Paris: Présence Africaine, 1983.

Césaire, Aimé. *Discours sur le Colonialisme*, Paris: Présence Africaine, 1955.

Churchill, Winston S. *The Second World War: Triumph and Tragedy*, Cambridge, Mass.: The Riverside Press, 1953.

Frutkin, Susan. *Aimé Césaire: Black Between Worlds*, Miami: University of Miami Center for Advanced International Studies, 1973.

Gilbert, Martin. *The Second World War*, New York: Henry Holt, 1989.

Kelley, Robin D.G., "A Poetics of Anticolonialism." *Monthly Review* 51 (November 1999): 1–21.

O'Ballance, Edgar. *The Algerian Insurrection, 1954–1962*, Hamden, Conn.: Archon Books, 1967.

Price, Richard. *The Convict and the Colonel*, Boston: Beacon Press, 1998.

Sartre, Jean-Paul. *Réflexions sur la Question Juive*, Paris: Paul Morihien, 1946. Trans. Georbe J. Becker. *Anti-Semite and Jew*, New York: Schocken Books, 1948.

Slater, Mariam K. *The Caribbean Family: Legitimacy in Martinique*, New York: St. Martin's Press, 1977.

Tauriac, Michel. *Les Années Créoles: La Catastrophe, La Fleur de la Passion, Sang Mêlés*, Paris: Omnibus, 1996.

INDEX

2/26

GAYLORD S

ML